# FABULOUS
## Chicken

Photographer: Rodrigo Gutiérrez
Food Stylist: Josée Robitaille
Graphic Design: Zapp

Props courtesy of: Stokes
                    Ramacieri Design Inc.
                    La Maison d'Émilie
                    Pier 1 Imports
                    Regal Ware Inc.

Pictured on the front cover: *Balsamic Chicken with Pears* (see recipe, p.136)

Design, photography and production by:
Brimar Publishing Inc.
338 Saint Antoine St. East
Montreal, Canada H2Y 1A3
Tel. (514) 954-1441
Fax (514) 954-5086

Recipes and manuscript © 1999 Fédération des producteurs de volailles du Québec
Photography © 1999 Brimar Publishing Inc.
All rights reserved.

The Fédération des producteurs de volailles du Québec is grateful to the Manitoba Chicken Producer Board and the Canadian Egg Marketing Agency for their recipe contributions and assistance.

Canadä

The publishers thank Heritage Canada for the support awarded under the Book Publishing Industry Development Program.

ISBN 2-89433-426-5
Printed in Canada

# FABULOUS
# Chicken

BRIMAR

# INTRODUCTION

Everybody loves chicken, and no wonder! It's delicious, nutritious, relatively inexpensive, and lends itself to a variety of wonderful cooking styles and techniques. Now there's a cookbook for those of us who can't get enough of this wonderful bird.

*Fabulous Chicken* is a collection of more than 120 up-to-date, tried and tested recipes from across the country. They represent the very best in simple and delicious main courses, side dishes and starters.

You'll find recipes for quick and easy everyday meals as well as main courses for special occasions, when nothing but the best will do! There is a whole chapter on chicken soups, including hearty old-fashioned favorites and exotic soups from around the world. You'll also find intriguing appetizers, delicious sandwiches and snacks, and a wonderful array of salads. Last but not least, we've included a dessert section featuring that other all-time favorite gift from the chicken – eggs.

From beginning to end, full-color photographs will make your mouth water and show you exactly how the completed dish can look. We have also included step-by-step photos of special techniques to make preparing these succulent dishes as easy as 1, 2, 3. Finally, you'll find helpful sections on stocks and sauces, basic cooking techniques, nutritional values, safe storage and handling methods.

# CONTENTS

Chicken is one of today's most popular and inexpensive foods. Low in calories and easy to digest, it is enjoyed just about everywhere. In fact, cooks around the world – from French to Chinese, Mexican to Italian – have discovered unique and wonderful ways to prepare this traditional favorite.

Here in North America, chicken has long held a place of honor at family gatherings. Think of a Sunday night dinner with a whole roasted chicken or an old-fashioned chicken and vegetable pie.

But until recently, preparing chicken at home was a somewhat time-consuming affair. The recipes in popular cookbooks from twenty years ago usually began with instructions to "clean and cut up a whole chicken." No wonder many cooks reserved chicken for special occasions!

By comparison, today's cooks have it easy. We can buy chicken whole or cut into serving pieces, skinless or boneless or both! We can even select between white and dark meat. Now, whether it's for a simple weekday dinner or an elegant feast, cooking chicken is quick and easy.

### *Popular modern cuts of chicken*

◀ *Boneless, skinless chicken breast halves and filets*

*Boneless, ▶ skinless chicken thighs and skinless chicken legs*

◀ *Chicken wings, whole and cut up*

With such convenience and so much variety, today's cook can literally prepare a chicken dinner in minutes!

Progress never stops, especially when it comes to finding new ways to please increasingly adventurous and demanding consumers. These are just some of the new cuts of chicken appearing on the market, all designed to make mealtime easier and more exciting.

## New cuts of chicken

Chicken ▶
breast
cutlets

Tournedos- ▶
style
chicken
breast
halves
and thighs

◀ Boneless
chicken leg
roast, plain
or stuffed

◀ Melon-shaped
boneless leg
roast, plain
or stuffed

Boneless ▶
chicken
breast
roast,
plain or
stuffed

Ground ▶
chicken,
white
or dark
meat

◀ Chicken
strips, white
or dark
meat

◀ Drumsticks
and
drumstick
cutlets

This cookbook contains several recipes featuring some of these exciting new cuts. If you can't yet find them at your local supermarket, ask your butcher whether they can be specially prepared for you.

# WHOLESOME
## _CHICKEN_

Dieticians and health experts agree that a healthy diet includes only modest amounts of fat from animal sources. For most of us, that means choosing lower-fat cuts of meat, and preparing them with little or no added fat. Fortunately, chicken fits easily into any healthy diet.

What's more, chicken contains a number of nutrients vital to health. It is an excellent source of complete protein, containing the full range of amino acids required for the growth, maintenance and repair of muscles and organs.

The niacin found in chicken aids digestion, and helps build and maintain healthy skin. Chicken is also a source of iron, zinc and phosphorous, which help build strong bones and teeth. As an added bonus, chicken is relatively low in cholesterol when compared to most cuts of beef, pork and lamb.

So all in all, chicken can play an important role in a healthy diet.

_Percentage of the recommended daily allowance of nutrients contained in 100 g (3½ oz) of cooked skinless chicken breast:_

| | |
|---|---|
| Niacin | 86% |
| Thiamin | 5% |
| Riboflavin | 7% |
| Pantothenic acid | 14% |
| Vitamin B6 | 33% |
| Vitamin B12 | 17% |
| Vitamin A | 5% |
| Zinc | 11% |
| Iron | 7% |
| Phosphorous | 21% |

from _Canadian Nutrient File, 1981_

_Chicken Pita Pockets with Celery Root, p. 76_          _Creamy Dijon Chicken, p. 148_

Nutritional value of chicken compared to selected cuts of red meat

| 100 grams (3½ oz), cooked | Fat (in grams) | Protein (in grams) | Calories |
|---|---|---|---|
| **Chicken** | | | |
| Breast, meat only | 2.1 | 33 | 159 |
| Leg, meat only | 6.9 | 25 | 170 |
| Lean ground chicken | 12.4* | 22 | 207 |
| **Beef** | | | |
| Sirloin steak | 6.7 | 29 | 186 |
| Inside round | 3.9 | 30 | 163 |
| Lean ground beef, well done | 13.9 | 28 | 245 |
| **Pork** | | | |
| Loin chop, center cut | 6.2 | 31 | 187 |
| Shoulder roast | 11.7 | 29 | 230 |

Sources: Chicken data: Moncton University Food Research Centre, 1996.
Pork data: University of Moncton, 1994
All other data: Canadian Nutrient File, 1991

All chicken and meat values are based on portions of 100 grams (approx. 3½ oz) trimmed of skin and visible fat.

*Maximum amount. Fat content varies depending on the kind of meat used.

*Chicken Satay with Peanut Sauce, p. 16*     *Asian-Style Glazed Chicken, p. 88*

*Grilled Chicken and Pesto Panini, p. 83*　　　*Japanese Wings, p. 33*

## BASIC TIPS FOR
### *COOKING CHICKEN*

Chicken should never be eaten raw or under-cooked. On the other hand, overcooked chicken tends to be dry and stringy. Boneless and skinless pieces, such as breasts and thighs, cook rapidly and are especially easy to overcook, so check them frequently.

The cooking times for recipes in this book are approximate, and will vary depending on the size of the pieces being cooked.

How to tell if a chicken is perfectly cooked? Boneless chicken pieces should be opaque white all the way through, with no tinge of pink. For chicken pieces on the bone, cut into the thickest part of the meat next to the bone. There should be no tinge of pink. For whole and half chickens, insert a sharp knife into the thickest part of the thigh. Juices should run clear, again with no tinge of pink.

## COOKING TECHNIQUES
### *A WORLD OF VARIETY*

The variety of methods for cooking chicken is nearly endless: it's delicious braised, barbecued, grilled, broiled, roasted, sautéed, steamed, simmered, stir-fried, poached, and fried. Here's a little refresher course on some of the more common techniques.

**Barbecued or grilled** chicken is cooked by direct heat, whether that heat comes from traditional wood coals, a gas grill, or the oven broiler. You can also grill chicken pieces in a special grill pan or a nonstick skillet.

**Braised** chicken involves first browning the chicken on all sides in a little oil or fat, then simmering it slowly, covered, over low heat with a small amount of liquid, usually stock or wine, and flavorings such as herbs and vegetables.

*Spicy Thai Chicken with Basil, p. 103*

*Roast Chicken with Port, p. 140*

**Broiling** is a good method for chicken halves, quarters and pieces. Either marinate the chicken first, or brush it lightly with melted butter or seasoned oil. Then cook it in the broiler pan about 6 inches (15 cm) from the element, turning the pieces halfway through.

**Frying** is a method of cooking in oil or fat. In shallow-frying, sautéeing and stir-frying, small boneless pieces are cooked in just enough oil to keep them from sticking to the pan. The drippings remaining in the pan can be simmered with stock, wine, cider or vinegar to make a sauce.

**Roasting** is a dry heat method of cooking without added fat or liquid, and is usually reserved for whole birds. Use a pan that is just a little larger than the bird itself, and place a rack in the pan so the chicken doesn't stew in its own juices. The roasting pan should not be tightly covered with a lid, but rather with a loose tent of foil.

**Simmering** involves cooking chicken slowly in a large amount of liquid flavored with herbs and seasonings; it's a technique often used for making soups. If you have a craving for chicken stew, simmer the chicken first, then cook the vegetables in the same cooking liquid, and add the reserved chicken at the last minute so it is not overcooked.

*Tropical Chicken Brochettes, p. 131*

*Crispy Baked Chicken Schnitzel, p. 96*

# HANDLING AND STORING
## *CHICKEN*

It is very important to handle all foods carefully, including chicken. If you remember to follow these simple steps for safe handling and storage, you shouldn't encounter any problems.

The first step takes place at the store. Check the packaging carefully for rips or leaks. Never buy chicken that is not properly wrapped. Above all, make sure the chicken is properly refrigerated or frozen, and check the "best before" date on the package.

At the check-out counter, make sure your chicken and meat products are packed separately from other foods, especially fresh produce. Otherwise meat juices may drip onto your fruits and vegetables during transport, and cause cross-contamination. Remember, even the most carefully prepared meats may contain a few bacteria that are harmless when cooked, but can cause serious illness if allowed to spread to raw foods or work surfaces.

### Safe storage

Once you've made your purchases, take your food straight home and refrigerate or freeze it immediately. Chicken and meat left to sit in a warm car will spoil quickly.

The storage chart on page 13 tells you exactly how long fresh and frozen chicken can be safely stored. If you do not anticipate that you will cook fresh chicken in the recommended time, freeze it immediately for later use.

Chicken should never be defrosted at room temperature. To thaw chicken out in the refrigerator, leave it in its original packaging and place it in a shallow dish to catch any drips. Calculate 5 hours thawing time for each pound (0.5 kg) of chicken. If you're in a hurry, place the chicken in its original packaging in enough cold water to cover it completely. Change the water frequently, and calculate 1 hour per pound (0.5 kg) of chicken.

To safely defrost chicken in your microwave, consult the owner's manual. Whichever method you choose, defrosted chicken should be cooked within 24 hours.

## Proper handling

When it's time to cook the chicken, make sure your hands have been washed in hot, soapy water and that your work surface is clean. Discard the wrapping from the chicken; do not reuse it.

When you have finished preparing the chicken, wash the cutting board with hot soapy water and rinse with a weak bleach solution. Do not reuse your cutting board or knives to prepare other foods without cleaning them first.

Once the chicken is cooked, place it on a clean plate. Never use the same dish that has touched raw chicken to hold cooked chicken. Cooked chicken can be held at room temperature for no longer than 1 hour. Otherwise, it should be kept warmer than 140°F (60°C), or colder than 39°F (4°C).

Remember, chill, clean, separate and cook and you'll never have to worry.

## Storage Time Chart for Chicken

|  | In refrigerator 39°F (4°C) | In freezer 0°F (-18°C) |
|---|---|---|
| Whole chicken | 1–3 days | 12 months |
| Chicken parts | 1–3 days | 6 months |
| Giblets | 1–2 days | 3–4 months |
| Ground chicken | 1 day | 2 months |
| Cooked pieces in sauce | 1–3 days | 3–6 months |
| Cooked pieces without sauce | 3–4 days | 1–3 months |

These are recommended storage times. Chicken frozen for longer is still safe to eat, but it may not be as juicy and tender.

# APPETIZERS

There's nothing like a delicious appetizer to introduce a fabulous meal! These light and savory morsels set the tone for the main course. Some of the recipes in this chapter offer new ways of combining chicken with a variety of fresh ingredients, while others feature chicken as the basis for unbeatable pâtés. The choice is yours!

Just remember that when it comes to appetizers, presentation is almost as important as the food itself. Use taste, texture and color to your advantage!

# CHICKEN SATAY
# WITH PEANUT SAUCE

*Preparation time: 5 minutes*
*Marinating time: 10 minutes*
*Cooking time: 10 minutes*
*4 to 6 servings*

| | | |
|---|---|---|
| 1 lb | boneless, skinless chicken breasts or thighs | 500 g |

**Marinade:**

| | | |
|---|---|---|
| 1 tsp | curry powder | 5 mL |
| 1 | garlic clove, finely chopped | 1 |
| 2 tbsp | soy sauce | 30 mL |
| 2 tbsp | lemon juice | 30 mL |
| 1 tbsp | sugar | 15 mL |

**Peanut Sauce:**

| | | |
|---|---|---|
| 3 tbsp | smooth peanut butter | 45 mL |
| 2 tbsp | liquid honey | 30 mL |
| 2 tbsp | soy sauce | 30 mL |
| 2 tbsp | water | 30 mL |
| | Tabasco sauce to taste | |

■ Cut chicken into 1 x 4-inch (2.5 x 10 cm) strips and place in shallow dish. Combine marinade ingredients and pour over chicken; cover and let marinate in refrigerator 10 to 60 minutes.

■ Place sauce ingredients in blender or food processor and process until smooth. If sauce separates, stir in 1 tbsp (15 mL) boiling water.

■ Thread chicken strips onto skewers. Cook on preheated, oiled barbecue rack over medium heat for 5 minutes each side, or until cooked.

■ Serve brochettes with a drizzle of peanut sauce, or use peanut sauce for dipping.

## CHICKEN AND BRIE
## FILO PACKETS

**Preparation time: 30 minutes**
**Cooking time: 25 minutes**
**6 servings**

| | | |
|---|---|---|
| I | leek, white part only, in julienne strips | I |
| ⅔ lb | ground chicken | 300 g |
| I | shallot, finely chopped | I |
| ¼ cup | chopped fresh fennel bulb | 50 mL |
| I | garlic clove, finely chopped | I |
| ⅓ lb | Brie cheese, rind removed | 150 g |
| 8 | chopped fresh mint leaves or I tsp (5 mL) dried mint | 8 |
| 9 | sheets filo pastry | 9 |
| ½ cup | melted butter | 125 mL |
| | salt and pepper | |

- Preheat oven to 400°F (200°C).
- Steam leek for 10 minutes. Drain well.
- In large bowl, combine leek, chicken, shallot, fennel, garlic, cheese and mint. Season with salt and pepper. Mix well.
- Arrange 1 sheet filo on work surface. Brush with butter. Top with second sheet and brush with butter. Top with third sheet and brush with butter. Cut triple layer in 4. Place ¼ cup (50 mL) of chicken mixture in center of each filo section. Wrap up to enclose filling and brush with more butter.
- Repeat with remaining 6 sheets of filo and chicken filling, to make a total of 12 packets.
- Place packets on greased baking sheet. Bake 20 to 25 minutes, or until golden-brown. Serve with a green salad, if desired.

Combine leek, chicken, shallot, fennel, garlic, cheese and mint.

Layer 3 sheets of filo pastry, brushing each one with butter.

Cut triple layer in 4. Place ¼ cup (50 mL) chicken mixture in center of each filo section.

Wrap pastry to enclose filling.

Brush each packet with more butter.

# CHICKEN, MOZZARELLA AND PEPPER TARTS

*Preparation time: 15 minutes*
*Cooking time: 30 minutes*
*Makes 24 small tarts*

| | | |
|---|---|---|
| 1 lb | ground chicken | 500 g |
| ¼ cup | finely chopped onion | 50 mL |
| ⅓ cup | finely chopped red bell pepper | 75 mL |
| 2 tbsp | finely chopped sun-dried tomatoes in oil | 30 mL |
| 2 tsp | dried basil | 10 mL |
| 2 cups | finely grated Mozzarella cheese | 500 mL |
| 24 | prepared mini-tart shells | 24 |

- Preheat oven to 350°F (180°C).

- In a nonstick skillet over medium-high heat, stir-fry the chicken just until it turns white. Add onion, pepper, tomatoes and basil. Continue cooking until onions are tender. Remove from heat and let cool.

- Stir cheese into cooled chicken mixture. Spoon mixture into tart shells. Bake 20 to 25 minutes or until pastry is golden brown and filling is bubbly.

# WESTERN-STYLE
# CHICKEN WINGS

*Preparation time: 20 minutes*
*Cooking time: 40 minutes*
*Makes 30-40 pieces*

| | | |
|---|---|---|
| 2 lbs | chicken wings | 1 kg |
| ½ cup | ketchup | 125 mL |
| ½ cup | chili sauce or salsa | 125 mL |
| 2 tbsp | honey | 30 mL |
| 1 tsp | Worcestershire sauce | 5 mL |
| ½ tsp | dry mustard powder | 2 mL |
| ¼ tsp | cayenne pepper | 1 mL |
| 1 | garlic clove, chopped | 1 |

- Preheat oven to 375°F (190°C).
- Cut off wing tips and reserve for stock, if desired. Split wings in two at joint.
- Combine all remaining ingredients to make a sauce. Coat chicken wings in sauce, and arrange in single layer on large, foil-covered baking sheet.
- Bake for 40 minutes, or until wings are tender.

# ARTICHOKES STUFFED WITH CHICKEN

**Preparation time: 15 minutes**
**Cooking time: 35 minutes**
**6 servings**

| | | |
|---|---|---|
| 6 | large fresh artichokes | 6 |
| ½ | lemon | ½ |
| 2 tbsp | butter | 30 mL |
| 1 lb | ground chicken | 500 g |
| 2 | shallots, finely chopped | 2 |
| 1 | green bell pepper, chopped | 1 |
| ½ | leek, white part only, thinly sliced | ½ |
| 2 | tomatoes, peeled and crushed | 2 |
| 1 cup | tomato sauce | 250 mL |
| 2 | garlic cloves, finely chopped | 2 |
| ⅓ cup | finely chopped fresh basil | 75 mL |
| | salt and pepper | |
| | pinch cayenne pepper or harissa | |

- Trim off the top quarter of artichokes, including leaf tips. Trim stem so artichokes sit flat. Pull off any discolored leaves. Rub all cut edges with lemon to prevent browning.
- Steam or cook artichokes in boiling salted water about 35 minutes, or until a leaf can easily be pulled out.
- Meanwhile, melt butter in skillet over medium-high heat. Add chicken, and stir-fry 4 minutes or until no longer pink.
- Add shallots. Cook 1 minute. Add green pepper and leek. Cook 4 minutes. Add tomatoes, tomato sauce and garlic; season with salt and pepper. Cook over low heat 10 minutes. Add basil and cayenne pepper; stir-fry 2 minutes.
- Drain artichokes upside-down. Open tops by spreading center leaves. Spoon out smallest leaves and hairy chokes.
- Fill artichoke cavities with chicken mixture. Keep warm until ready to serve.

**Note:** *Instead of artichokes, you can stuff the chicken mixture into hollowed-out tomatoes or bell peppers. You can also substitute fresh basil with basil pesto.*

# BARBECUED CHICKEN AND VEGETABLE MINI-PIZZAS

**Preparation time: 20 minutes**
**Cooking time: 8 minutes**
**4 servings**

| | | |
|---|---|---|
| ½ lb | boneless, skinless chicken breast | 250 g |
| ¼ cup | Italian-style dressing | 50 mL |
| 1 | red bell pepper | 1 |
| 1 | zucchini | 1 |
| 1 | tomato | 1 |
| 1 | onion | 1 |
| 2 | 7-inch (18 cm) pre-cooked pizza shells | 2 |
| 1 cup | grated Mozzarella or Fontina cheese | 250 mL |
| ¼ cup | chopped fresh basil | 50 mL |

■ Marinate chicken a few minutes in Italian dressing. Pat dry and cook on preheated barbecue 5 to 7 minutes each side, until no longer pink inside. Let cool. Cut into thin strips and set aside.

■ Meanwhile, grill red pepper until blackened on all sides. Place in paper bag until cool. Remove skin, seeds and membranes. Cut in strips and set aside.

■ Slice zucchini in long strips lengthwise. Grill 1 to 2 minutes each side. Cut in 1-inch (2.5 cm) pieces. Set aside.

■ Dice tomato and onion and sprinkle over pizza shells. Add chicken and zucchini. Sprinkle with cheese and basil. Add red pepper strips.

■ Place pizza on barbecue grill rack and cook uncovered over medium-high heat for 2 to 3 minutes, or until bottom crust is lightly browned. Slide pizza onto baking sheet. Place baking sheet on barbecue, and close barbecue lid. Cook 5 minutes or until cheese bubbles and crust is crisp as desired.

# FRESH HERB AND CHICKEN PÂTÉ

*Preparation time: 15 minutes*
*Cooking time: 15 minutes*
*Makes about 3 cups (750 mL)*

| | | |
|---|---|---|
| 1½ cups | softened butter | 375 mL |
| 1 | onion, chopped | 1 |
| 1-2 | garlic cloves, chopped | 1-2 |
| 1 lb | chicken livers, trimmed | 500 g |
| 1 tsp | *each* fresh chopped thyme, chives, marjoram and tarragon | 5 mL |
| 3 tbsp | port or sherry (optional) | 45 mL |

- Melt ⅓ cup (75 mL) of butter in a skillet. Add onion and cook over low heat until soft and translucent. Add garlic and cook a few minutes more. Remove from skillet and set aside.

- In same skillet, stir-fry chicken livers over medium-high heat until barely pink inside.

- Place chicken livers, onion mixture and remaining butter in food processor or blender. Process until smooth. Add chopped herbs and port; mix well.

- Pack into individual ramekins or a 4-cup (1 L) serving dish. Refrigerate 1 day before serving.

# CABBAGE ROLLS
# WITH CHICKEN

*Preparation time: 15 minutes*
*Cooking time: 45 minutes*
*6 servings*

| | | |
|---|---|---|
| 1 | medium Savoy cabbage | 1 |
| 3 | slices wholewheat bread, crusts removed | 3 |
| ½ cup | milk | 125 mL |
| 1 lb | ground chicken | 500 g |
| 1 | garlic clove, finely chopped | 1 |
| 1 | egg | 1 |
| 1 | shallot, finely chopped | 1 |
| 1 tsp | crushed dill seed | 5 mL |
| 3 | chopped mushrooms | 3 |
| | salt and pepper | |

- Preheat oven to 400°F (200°C).

- Break off 6 large whole cabbage leaves. Cook in boiling salted water 2 minutes. Drain and cut out hard stalks; set leaves aside.

- In a bowl, soak bread in milk 1 to 2 minutes to soften. Add chicken, garlic, egg, shallot, dill seed and mushrooms. Season to taste with salt and pepper. Mix well.

- Place about ⅓ cup (75 mL) in center of each cabbage leaf and wrap up to make oblong rolls.

- Place rolls in a deep casserole or baking dish; add 1 cup (250 mL) hot water.

- Cover and bake 40 minutes. Serve hot with tomato relish or other condiments of your choice.

*Cook cabbage leaves in boiling salted water 2 minutes. Drain.*

*Cut out hard stalks; set leaves aside.*

*To bread and milk, add chicken, garlic, egg, shallot, dill seed and mushrooms. Season and mix well.*

④

Place about ⅓ cup (75 mL) in center of each cabbage leaf.

⑤

Fold cabbage over filling.

⑥

Fold in ends and roll to make oblong packages.

## OLD-FASHIONED CHICKEN PÂTÉ

*Preparation time: 10 minutes*
*Cooking time: 1½ hours*
*Makes about 4 cups (1L)*

| | | |
|---|---|---|
| 1 lb | ground chicken | 500 g |
| 1 cup | diced fresh bread (without crusts) | 250 mL |
| 1 cup | milk | 250 mL |
| 1½ cups | chicken stock | 375 mL |
| 1 | large onion, chopped | 1 |
| 1 | garlic clove, chopped | 1 |
| 2 tsp | dry mustard powder | 10 mL |
| 1 tsp | salt | 5 mL |
| 1 tsp | dried parsley | 5 mL |
| 1 tsp | tomato paste | 5 mL |
| | pinch dried thyme | |
| | pinch ground cloves | |

- Combine all ingredients in a saucepan. Bring to a boil, stirring constantly.
- Reduce heat to very low and let cook about 1½ hours, or until liquid has completely evaporated.
- Pack mixture into individual ramekins or a large serving dish.
- Serve with crusty bread or crackers.

# CHICKEN
# AU GRATIN

***Preparation time: 5 minutes***
***Cooking time: 10 minutes***
***4 servings***

| | | |
|---|---|---|
| 4 | slices tomato, quartered | 4 |
| ½ cup | chopped cooked chicken | 125 mL |
| 4 | green onions, chopped | 4 |
| 1 tsp | dried basil or tarragon | 5 mL |
| 4 tbsp | heavy cream (35%) or sour cream | 60 mL |
| 4 | eggs | 4 |
| | butter | |
| | grated Parmesan cheese | |
| | salt and pepper | |

- Preheat oven to 350°F (180°C). Butter 4 ramekins or small pyrex dishes and sprinkle lightly with Parmesan cheese.

- Arrange tomato pieces, chicken and green onion over Parmesan in each ramekin. Sprinkle with basil; season with salt and pepper. Top with cream.

- Break egg onto center of chicken layer in each ramekin. Sprinkle with a little more Parmesan.

- Bake 10 to 15 minutes, or until eggs are cooked as desired.

# TANDOORI CHICKEN
# KEBABS

*Preparation time: 20 minutes*
*Marinating time: 4 hours*
*Cooking time: 10 minutes*
*4 servings*

| | | |
|---|---|---|
| 1 lb | boneless, skinless chicken breasts or thighs | 500 g |
| 8 to 12 | wooden skewers | 8 to 12 |

## Marinade:

| | | |
|---|---|---|
| 1 cup | plain yogurt | 250 mL |
| 1 tbsp | fresh lemon juice | 15 mL |
| 1 | garlic clove, finely chopped | 1 |
| 1 | small onion, finely chopped | 1 |
| 1½ tsp | curry powder | 7 mL |
| 1 tsp | ground cumin | 5 mL |
| 1 tsp | ground coriander | 5 mL |
| 1 tsp | ground ginger | 5 mL |
| ½ tsp | salt | 2 mL |

## Tandoori Sauce:

| | | |
|---|---|---|
| 1 cup | heavy cream (35%) | 250 mL |
| ½ cup | dry white wine or chicken stock | 125 mL |
| 3 tbsp | tomato paste | 45 mL |
| 1 tsp | curry powder | 5 mL |
| ½ tsp | ground coriander | 2 mL |
| ½ tsp | ground cumin | 2 mL |
| ½ tsp | garam masala* | 2 mL |
| ½ cup | chopped fresh cilantro (optional) | 125 mL |

- Cut chicken into large bite-sized cubes and thread onto skewers. Place skewers in a large sealable plastic bag. Combine marinade ingredients and pour over chicken, making sure each piece is well coated. Close bag and refrigerate at least 4 hours.

- Combine all ingredients for Tandoori Sauce except fresh cilantro. Refrigerate in air-tight container until ready to use.

- Preheat barbecue grill to medium heat. Remove chicken from marinade and place on grill. Discard bag and leftover marinade.

- Grill chicken, with barbecue lid down, about 10 minutes or until chicken is no longer pink inside and juices run clear. Turn skewers at least 3 times during cooking.

- While chicken is grilling, transfer Tandoori Sauce to a medium saucepan. Bring sauce to a slow boil, stirring constantly, then reduce heat to low. Simmer until sauce is slightly thickened, stirring occasionally. Cover saucepan and keep warm until chicken is cooked.

- Transfer chicken to a serving platter. Drizzle sauce over kebabs. If desired, sprinkle with fresh cilantro just before serving.

*You can find garam masala at Asian specialty food stores, or substitute ½ tsp (2 mL) cinnamon.*

# HERB AND CHICKEN CROQUETTES

*Preparation time: 15 minutes*
*Cooking time: 10 minutes*
*Makes about 4 dozen*

| | | |
|---|---|---:|
| 1 lb | ground chicken | 500 g |
| 2 | eggs, beaten | 2 |
| ½ cup | dry breadcrumbs | 125 mL |
| 2 tbsp | grated Parmesan cheese | 30 mL |
| 1 tbsp | dried parsley | 15 mL |
| 2 tsp | dried basil | 10 mL |
| 2 tsp | dried oregano | 10 mL |
| ½ tsp | garlic powder | 2 mL |
| | salt and pepper to taste | |
| | peanut oil | |
| | cantaloupe, cut in cubes, if desired | |

- In large mixing bowl, combine all ingredients except oil and cantaloupe; mix well. Shape into small balls about 1 inch (2.5 cm) in diameter.
- Pour about ⅛-inch (3 mm) oil into a skillet over medium heat. When oil is hot, add chicken balls, in batches if necessary, and cook about 5 minutes on each side until golden.
- Drain on paper towels and keep warm until ready to serve.
- Serve hot on toothpicks with cantaloupe, if desired.

**Tip:** Chicken croquettes can be prepared ahead of time and refrigerated, covered, for up to 2 days.

## JAPANESE WINGS

*Preparation time: 15 minutes*
*Marinating time: 2 hours*
*Cooking time: 15 minutes*
*Makes about 40 wings*

| | | |
|---|---|---|
| 5 lbs | chicken wings | 2.5 kg |
| 1 cup | soy sauce | 250 mL |
| ¼ cup | sugar | 50 mL |
| 1 tsp | ground ginger | 5 mL |
| 2 | garlic cloves, finely chopped | 2 |
| ½ cup | toasted sesame seeds | 125 mL |

- Cut off wing tips and reserve for stock, if desired.

- Combine soy sauce, sugar, ginger and garlic in a large dish. Reserve ¼-cup (50 mL) of mixture for basting. Marinate wings in remaining soy mixture at least 2 hours in refrigerator, turning wings occasionally.

- Discard marinade and arrange wings in single layer on broiler pan. Place pan 6 inches (15 cm) from broiler element and broil about 10 minutes. Turn wings, baste with reserved soy mixture and continue cooking another 5 to 10 minutes, until browned and tender.

- Sprinkle with sesame seeds and serve hot.

# CHICKEN LIVER AND APPLE PÂTÉ

*Preparation time: 10 minutes*
*Cooking time: 25 minutes*
*Makes about 2 cups (500 mL)*

| | | |
|---|---|---|
| ½ cup | butter | 125 mL |
| 1 | large onion, chopped | 1 |
| 2 | garlic cloves, crushed | 2 |
| 2 | medium apples, peeled, cored and chopped | 2 |
| 1 lb | chicken livers, trimmed | 500 g |
| ¼ cup | Calvados, cognac or apple juice | 50 mL |
| 1 tsp | Dijon mustard | 5 mL |
| ½ tsp | salt | 2 mL |
| 1 tsp | dried thyme | 5 mL |
| ½ tsp | ground nutmeg | 2 mL |
| ¼ tsp | ground black pepper | 1 mL |
| ⅛ tsp | cayenne pepper | 0.5 mL |

- Melt 2 tbsp (30 mL) butter in a large skillet over medium heat. Add onion and cook, stirring occasionally, until soft, about 10 minutes.

- Add garlic and apples; cook, stirring constantly, 3 to 5 minutes or until apples are tender. Place mixture in food processor or blender.

- To same skillet, add another 2 tbsp (30 mL) butter. Add chicken livers and cook 5 minutes, stirring constantly. Add Calvados, cover and continue cooking until livers are no longer pink inside, about 5 minutes.

- Add livers with cooking liquid to food processor. Add remaining butter along with mustard, salt, herbs and spices. Process until smooth. Pack mixture into a serving dish and refrigerate 1 day before serving.

- Serve with crusty bread or crackers.

*Add garlic and apples; cook, stirring constantly, 3 to 5 minutes.*

*Cook chicken livers in butter 5 minutes, stirring constantly.*

*Add Calvados, cover and continue cooking until livers are no longer pink inside.*

Add livers with cooking liquid to food processor.

Add remaining butter along with mustard, salt, herbs and spices.

Pack mixture into a serving dish and refrigerate 1 day.

# SPRING ROLLS WITH CHICKEN AND SHRIMP

*Preparation time: 30 minutes*
*Cooking time: 5 minutes*
*6 servings*

## Dipping Sauce:

| | | |
|---|---|---|
| ¼ cup | fresh lemon or lime juice | 50 mL |
| ¼ cup | Asian-style fish sauce (nuoc mam) | 50 mL |
| 1 tbsp | rice vinegar | 15 mL |
| 1 tbsp | sugar | 15 mL |
| 1 tsp | finely chopped fresh ginger (optional) | 5 mL |
| 1 | garlic clove, finely chopped | 1 |
| | pinch cayenne pepper (optional) | |

## Spring Rolls:

| | | |
|---|---|---|
| 4 oz | rice vermicelli | 120 g |
| 12 | 8-inch (20 cm) round spring roll wrappers | 12 |
| 18 | large cooked shrimp, halved lengthwise | 18 |
| 1 cup | diced cooked chicken | 250 mL |
| 1 cup | bean sprouts | 250 mL |
| 1 | cucumber, peeled, seeded and grated | 1 |
| 1 | carrot, peeled and finely grated | 1 |
| | thinly shredded lettuce leaves | |
| | fresh whole cilantro or mint leaves | |

- Combine all sauce ingredients in a bowl until smooth. Let stand about 30 minutes to combine flavors.

- Meanwhile, soak vermicelli in hot water 10 minutes. Drain, then place in boiling water. Cook a few minutes, until just tender. Rinse in cold water and drain well.

- One at a time, soak spring roll wrappers for a few seconds in hot water, until soft. Remove from water and place flat on work surface.

- On each wrapper, arrange 3 shrimp halves. Divide chicken, beansprouts, cucumber, carrot, lettuce and vermicelli evenly over shrimp. Top with a few cilantro or mint leaves.

- Fold one side of wrapper over mixture. Fold in one of the ends and roll carefully.

- Wrap spring rolls in damp cloth and refrigerate.

- Strain dipping sauce and serve at room temperature with cold spring rolls.

**Tip:** You can use different vegetables such as julienne green onions, thinly sliced mushrooms, slivered red and yellow bell peppers, or shredded green cabbage.

# SALADS

Salads add a touch of color and freshness to a meal, any time of year. And you would be surprised at the results when you combine fruits and vegetables with meat, or hot with cold ingredients.

Whether it's an easy chicken twist on traditional favorites like Caesar or Greek salad, or a whole new taste sensation like *Mango Chicken and Spinach Salad*, the recipes in this chapter are sure to please everyone.

# WARM CHICKEN LIVER SALAD WITH LEMON DRESSING

*Preparation time: 15 minutes*
*Cooking time: 20 minutes*
*4 servings*

## Lemon Dressing:

| 2 tsp | grated lemon zest | 10 mL |
|---|---|---|
| ¼ cup | lemon juice | 50 mL |
| ½ tsp | salt | 2 mL |
| 1 tsp | fresh thyme | 5 mL |
| ⅛ tsp | pepper | 0.5 mL |
| ½ cup | extra virgin olive oil | 125 mL |

## Salad:

| 4 cups | mixed lettuce leaves, washed and torn | 1L |
|---|---|---|
| 4 | slices bacon | 4 |
| 1 lb | chicken livers, trimmed | 500 g |
| ¼ tsp | pepper | 1 mL |
| 1½ cups | quartered fresh mushrooms | 375 mL |

- In a small bowl, stir together all dressing ingredients except oil. Gradually add oil in a thin stream, whisking constantly. Set aside.

- Place lettuce in a large bowl.

- Cook bacon in medium skillet over medium-high heat until crisp. Drain bacon on paper towels and crumble; set aside.

- Drain all but 1 tbsp (15 mL) grease from skillet. Add chicken livers and cook over medium-high heat about 10 minutes, stirring occasionally. Sprinkle in pepper. Remove livers from skillet. Keep warm in oven.

- To same skillet, add mushrooms. Cook 5 minutes. Add to livers.

- Pour half the lemon dressing over chicken livers and toss lightly. Pour remaining dressing over lettuce and toss.

- Divide lettuce among 4 salad plates. Top with warm livers and mushrooms. Sprinkle with bacon and serve.

# GREEK SALAD WITH CHICKEN

*Preparation time: 15 minutes*
*Cooking time: 5 minutes*
*4 servings*

| | | |
|---|---|---|
| 3 | pita bread rounds, cut into 1-inch (2.5 cm) pieces | 3 |
| ½ lb | Feta cheese | 250 g |
| 2 cups | diced cooked chicken | 500 mL |
| 1 | English cucumber, peeled, seeded and diced | 1 |
| 3 | tomatoes, cubed | 3 |
| 4 | green onions, thinly sliced | 4 |
| 1 | small head Romaine lettuce, washed and torn | 1 |

**Dressing:**

| | | |
|---|---|---|
| 2 tbsp | fresh lemon juice | 30 mL |
| 2 tbsp | red wine vinegar | 30 mL |
| 1 tsp | salt | 5 mL |
| ½ tsp | pepper | 2 mL |
| ½ tsp | dried oregano | 2 mL |
| ¼ cup | olive oil | 50 mL |
| ¼ cup | chopped fresh parsley | 50 mL |
| 2 tbsp | chopped fresh mint | 30 mL |

- Preheat oven to 350°F (180°C). Arrange pita pieces in single layer on ungreased cookie sheet. Bake 5 minutes.
- Crumble Feta cheese into ½-inch (1 cm) pieces.
- In large bowl, combine pita pieces, Feta and remaining salad ingredients.
- Stir together dressing ingredients and pour over salad. Toss gently to coat.

## CHICKEN AND CARROT SALAD

**Preparation time: 10 minutes**
**6 servings**

| | | |
|---|---|---|
| 3 cups | diced cooked chicken | 750 mL |
| 2 cups | grated carrots | 500 mL |
| ¾ cup | orange segments or apple wedges | 175 mL |
| ¾ cup | golden raisins | 175 mL |
| ¾ cup | plain yogurt or light sour cream | 175 mL |
| 1 tsp | fresh lemon juice | 5 mL |
| 1 tsp | liquid honey | 5 mL |
| ½ tsp | salt | 2 mL |
| ¼ tsp | finely ground pepper | 1 mL |
| ½ cup | toasted almonds | 125 mL |
| | frisée lettuce leaves | |

- Combine chicken, carrots and oranges in a large bowl.
- In a second bowl, soak raisins in boiling water for 5 minutes. Drain and pat dry with paper towels. Add to chicken mixture.
- Stir together yogurt, lemon juice, honey, salt and pepper. Pour over chicken mixture and stir to combine.
- Serve on lettuce leaves and garnish with almonds.

# FRUITY CHICKEN AND
# FUSILLI SALAD

**Preparation time: 15 minutes**
**2 servings**

| | | |
|---|---|---|
| I cup | tricolor fusilli pasta, cooked | 250 mL |
| I cup | cubed barbecued chicken | 250 mL |
| ½ | orange, in segments, membranes removed | ½ |
| ½ | ruby grapefruit, in segments, membranes removed | ½ |
| ¼ cup | raisins | 50 mL |
| ¼ cup | pecans or cashews | 50 mL |
| | Romaine or Boston lettuce | |

**Dressing:**

| | | |
|---|---|---|
| I tbsp | Dijon mustard | 15 mL |
| I tbsp | walnut oil | 15 mL |
| 2 tsp | white wine vinegar | 10 mL |
| 2 tsp | cold water | 10 mL |
| | salt and pepper to taste | |

- Line individual plates with lettuce.
- Combine remaining salad ingredients in a large bowl.
- Mix together dressing ingredients and pour over salad. Toss well and serve.

# MIXED GREENS WITH CHICKEN AND AVOCADO

**Preparation time: 15 minutes**
**2 servings**

| | | |
|---|---|---|
| 3 cups | mixed lettuce leaves (Boston, radicchio, frisée, endive) | 750 mL |
| 1 | avocado, peeled and sliced | 1 |
| ½ | red onion, cut in rings | ½ |
| 1 cup | barbecued chicken strips | 250 mL |
| ½ | red or yellow bell pepper, cut in strips | ½ |
| | toasted cashews or almonds | |

**Dressing:**

| | | |
|---|---|---|
| ½ cup | plain yogurt | 125 mL |
| 1 tbsp | liquid honey | 15 mL |
| 1 tbsp | chopped fresh basil | 15 mL |
| | juice of ½ orange | |
| | salt and pepper to taste | |

- Place all salad ingredients in a large bowl.
- Combine dressing ingredients. Add to salad and toss.

# CHICKEN SALAD NIÇOISE

*Preparation time: 30 minutes*
*Cooking time: 10 minutes*
*4 servings*

| | | |
|---|---|---|
| I lb | boneless, skinless chicken breasts or thighs | 500 g |
| 2 tbsp | olive oil | 30 mL |
| ½ tsp | salt | 2 mL |
| ¼ tsp | pepper | I mL |
| ½ tsp | chopped fresh rosemary | 2 mL |
| I lb | small new potatoes, cooked, halved and chopped | 500 g |
| ½ lb | green beans, trimmed, cooked 3 minutes | 250 g |
| 3 | hard-boiled eggs, cut in wedges | 3 |
| 3 | tomatoes, cut in wedges | 3 |
| ½ cup | pitted black olives | 125 mL |
| ½ tsp | chopped fresh or dried tarragon | 2 mL |
| ¼ cup | chopped fresh basil or parsley | 50 mL |

**Dressing:**

| | | |
|---|---|---|
| 3 tbsp | red wine vinegar | 45 mL |
| I tsp | anchovy paste | 5 mL |
| 2 | garlic cloves, finely chopped | 2 |
| ½ tsp | pepper | 2 mL |
| ½ cup | olive oil | 125 mL |

- Pat chicken dry with paper towels. Stir together oil, salt, pepper and rosemary. Place chicken in oil mixture.

- Cook chicken on oiled barbecue grill over medium heat 5 to 7 minutes on each side, or until cooked through. Let cool and cut into strips.

- Place potatoes in middle of a large, shallow serving bowl. Surround potatoes with a ring of green beans, then eggs and tomatoes. Top potatoes with grilled chicken. Sprinkle with olives, tarragon and basil.

- Stir together dressing ingredients and pour over salad just before serving.

# CANTONESE-STYLE CHICKEN SALAD

**Preparation time: 15 minutes**
**6 servings**

| | | |
|---|---|---|
| 2 tbsp | chopped fresh ginger | 30 mL |
| 1 tbsp | sesame oil | 15 mL |
| 2 tbsp | vegetable oil | 30 mL |
| 2 tbsp | soy sauce | 30 mL |
| 1 tbsp | lemon juice | 15 mL |
| 2 cups | diced cooked chicken | 500 mL |
| 1 | can (10 oz/284 mL) water chestnuts, drained and quartered | 1 |
| 4 | green onions, chopped | 4 |
| 1 | cucumber, cut in 4 and thinly sliced | 1 |
| ½ | red bell pepper, thinly sliced | ½ |
| 6 | baby corns, halved | 6 |
| 1 cup | chopped bean sprouts | 250 mL |
| | salt and pepper | |

■ In a small bowl, combine ginger, sesame oil, vegetable oil, soy sauce and lemon juice; season with salt and pepper.

■ In a medium bowl, mix together remaining ingredients. Pour in first mixture and toss gently until ingredients are well coated. Garnish with baby corns.

**Tip:** Serve salad in small bowls or stuff into hollowed-out tomatoes, bell peppers or zucchini.

# MANGO CHICKEN
# AND SPINACH SALAD

*Preparation time: 15 minutes*
*2 servings*

| | | |
|---|---|---|
| 3 cups | fresh spinach leaves, washed and drained | 750 mL |
| ¼ cup | toasted pine nuts | 50 mL |
| ½ | mango, peeled, pitted and cut into pieces | ½ |
| 1 cup | barbecued chicken, chopped | 250 mL |
| | fresh tarragon for garnish | |

**Orange Dressing:**

| | | |
|---|---|---|
| 1 | small garlic clove, finely chopped | 1 |
| 1 tbsp | lemon juice | 15 mL |
| ¼ cup | freshly squeezed orange juice | 50 mL |
| 1 tsp | Dijon mustard | 5 mL |
| ½ tsp | sugar | 2 mL |
| ½ tsp | white wine vinegar | 2 mL |
| 2 tbsp | olive oil | 30 mL |
| | salt and pepper | |

- Combine all salad ingredients except chicken and tarragon.

- Mix together all dressing ingredients except oil. Gradually whisk in oil; season with salt and pepper. Pour dressing over spinach mixture. Toss well.

- Divide salad between 2 plates. Place chicken in center over salad. Garnish with fresh tarragon.

49

# CHICKEN AND PASTA SALAD
# WITH GRILLED VEGETABLES

*Preparation time: 20 minutes*
*Cooking time: 4 minutes*
*4 servings*

| | | |
|---|---|---|
| ½ | eggplant (about ½ lb/250 g) | ½ |
| 2 | zucchini | 2 |
| I | large onion | I |
| 2 | red bell peppers | 2 |
| ¼ cup | olive oil | 50 mL |
| I | garlic clove, finely chopped | I |
| ½ tsp | salt | 2 mL |
| ½ tsp | pepper | 2 mL |
| ⅓ lb | penne pasta, cooked and drained | 150 g |
| 2 cups | diced cooked chicken | 500 mL |

**Dressing:**

| | | |
|---|---|---|
| ⅓ cup | balsamic vinegar | 75 mL |
| 2 tbsp | red wine vinegar | 30 mL |
| 2 | garlic cloves, finely chopped | 2 |
| I tsp | Dijon mustard | 5 mL |
| I½ tsp | salt | 7 mL |
| ½ tsp | pepper | 2 mL |
| ⅓ cup | olive oil | 150 mL |
| ¼ cup | chopped fresh basil or parsley | 50 mL |
| ¼ cup | chopped fresh chives or green onions | 50 mL |

- Slice eggplant, zucchini and onion ½-inch (1 cm) thick. Cut peppers in half and remove seeds and membranes.
- Combine oil, garlic, salt and pepper. Add to vegetables and toss gently.
- Grill eggplant, zucchini and onion on barbecue or under broiler until lightly browned on both sides, about 4 to 5 minutes. Meanwhile, grill red peppers, skin side to heat, until skin is blackened. Let cool, then peel.
- Cut all vegetables into 1-inch (2.5 cm) pieces and place in large bowl. Add chicken and pasta.
- Combine dressing ingredients. Add to pasta, chicken and vegetables; toss and serve.

## CHICKEN TABOULÉ

*Preparation time: 15 minutes*
*Chilling time: 1 hour*
*4 servings*

| | | |
|---|---|---|
| 2 cups | diced cooked chicken | 500 mL |
| 2 cups | cooked barley | 500 mL |
| 1 tsp | ground cumin | 5 mL |
| ½ tsp | ground coriander | 2 mL |
| 2 | medium tomatoes, peeled, seeded and diced | 2 |
| 2 tbsp | fresh lemon juice | 30 mL |
| 2 tbsp | extra virgin olive oil | 30 mL |
| 1 | green onion, chopped | 1 |
| 1 cup | diced peeled cucumber | 250 mL |
| ¼ cup | chopped fresh parsley | 50 mL |
| 2 tbsp | chopped fresh cilantro | 30 mL |

- In a large bowl, mix together all ingredients. Chill at least 1 hour.
- Serve on lettuce leaves or in pita bread pockets with shredded lettuce, if desired.

# CHICKEN
# CAESAR SALAD

**Preparation time: 10 minutes**
**4 servings**

| | | |
|---|---|---:|
| 2 cups | diced cooked chicken | 500 mL |
| 2 | tomatoes, cut in wedges | 2 |
| 1 cup | croutons | 250 mL |
| 8 | slices bacon, cooked and diced | 8 |
| 6 cups | torn Romaine lettuce | 1.5 L |
| 2 tbsp | chopped fresh parsley | 30 mL |

## Dressing:

| | | |
|---|---|---:|
| ½ cup | mayonnaise | 125 mL |
| 2 | garlic cloves, finely chopped | 2 |
| 1 tbsp | *each* anchovy paste, Worcestershire sauce, fresh lemon juice and red wine vinegar | 15 mL |
| ¼ tsp | Tabasco sauce | 1 mL |
| ¼ tsp | pepper | 1 mL |
| ¼ cup | olive oil | 50 mL |
| ½ cup | grated Parmesan cheese | 125 mL |

- In a salad bowl, place chicken, tomatoes, croutons, bacon, lettuce and parsley.
- Combine dressing ingredients in food processor or blender; process until smooth and creamy.
- Pour dressing over salad and toss gently.

# SOUPS

**F**ew foods are as comforting and nutritious as good old chicken soup. But this chapter gives 'chicken soup' a whole new meaning! Whether you're looking for a hot cup of soup to warm up to a winter meal, or an exotic meal in a bowl, this chapter has it all.

Starting with chicken or chicken stock, there's no end to the variety of sumptuous soups you can make in minutes. Here are just a few of our favorites.

# HOT THAI SOUP

*Preparation time: 15 minutes*
*Cooking time: 10 minutes*
*4 to 6 servings*

| | | |
|---|---|---|
| 2½ cups | chicken stock | 625 mL |
| 1 cup | coconut milk | 250 mL |
| 1 | stalk lemongrass, peeled and sliced | 1 |
| 1 | garlic clove, finely chopped | 1 |
| ¼ tsp | Sambal Oelek* or cayenne pepper | 1 mL |
| 2 cups | diced cooked chicken | 500 mL |
| 1 | medium carrot, peeled and grated | 1 |
| 2 cups | shredded fresh spinach | 500 mL |
| 2 | green onions, sliced diagonally | 2 |
| ¼ cup | chopped fresh Thai basil or cilantro | 50 mL |

- In a medium saucepan, combine stock, coconut milk, lemongrass and garlic. Cover and cook 10 minutes over medium-high heat.
- Add Sambal Oelek, chicken, carrot and spinach. Cover and continue cooking 5 minutes.
- Add green onions and Thai basil just before serving.

*\* Sambal Oelek is a type of sauce made from hot peppers, available at Asian specialty food stores.*

## VIETNAMESE NOODLE SOUP

**Preparation time: 10 minutes**
**Cooking time: 10 minutes**
**4 servings**

| | | |
|---|---|---|
| 3 cups | chicken stock | 750 mL |
| 1 tbsp | oyster sauce | 15 mL |
| 2 tsp | nuoc mam sauce* | 10 mL |
| 1 cup | rice vermicelli, soaked in water and drained | 250 mL |
| 2 | carrots, sliced | 2 |
| ¼ lb | cooked chicken, cut in strips | 125 g |
| ½ cup | thinly sliced mushrooms | 125 mL |
| 3 | green onions, thinly sliced | 3 |
| 1 | garlic clove, finely chopped | 1 |
| | salt and pepper | |
| | fresh mint leaves | |

■ Place chicken stock, oyster sauce and nuoc mam sauce in large saucepan. Bring to a boil.

■ Add vermicelli and carrots; cook 3 to 4 minutes.

■ Add chicken strips, mushrooms, green onions and garlic. Continue cooking 3 minutes.

■ Season with salt and pepper; serve in large bowls, garnished with mint.

*Nuoc mam sauce is a Vietnamese condiment made from fish. It is a good flavoring for soups and stews, and is available at Asian specialty food stores.

# CREAM OF BROCCOLI

*Preparation time: 10 minutes*
*Cooking time: 25 minutes*
*6 servings*

| | | |
|---|---|---|
| 1 tbsp | butter | 15 mL |
| 1 | onion, finely chopped | 1 |
| 1 cup | sliced leek (green and white parts) | 250 mL |
| 3 cups | chicken stock, skimmed | 750 mL |
| 1 cup | chopped broccoli (stems and florets) | 250 mL |
| 1 | medium potato, cubed | 1 |
| ½ cup | milk | 125 mL |
| 2 tbsp | chopped fresh chives or parsley | 30 mL |
| ½ tsp | *each* dry mustard powder and thyme (optional) | 2 mL |
| | salt and pepper | |
| | heavy cream (35%) | |

- Melt butter in a large saucepan over medium heat. Add onion and leek; sauté until tender.
- Add chicken stock, broccoli and potato. Bring to a boil. Cover and let simmer over medium heat until vegetables are tender.
- Purée in blender or food processor. Return to saucepan and add milk, chives, dry mustard and thyme. Season with salt and pepper.
- Reheat and serve, topped with cream and garnished with fresh chives, if desired.

# CHICKEN
# RICE SOUP

*Preparation time: 10 minutes*
*Cooking time: 35 minutes*
*4 servings*

| | | |
|---|---|---|
| 6 cups | chicken stock | 1.5 L |
| ½ cup | rice | 125 mL |
| 2 | celery stalks, sliced | 2 |
| 1 | carrot, sliced | 1 |
| 1 cup | sliced mushrooms | 250 mL |
| 1 cup | diced cooked chicken | 250 mL |
| 1 cup | frozen peas | 250 mL |
| 4 | green onions, chopped | 4 |
| 1 tbsp | chopped fresh thyme | 15 mL |
| | salt and pepper | |

- In a medium saucepan, bring chicken stock to a boil. Add rice and cook over medium heat 15 minutes. Add celery, carrot and mushrooms. Cook about 10 minutes.

- Add chicken, peas, onions and thyme. Lower heat and let simmer 5 minutes.

- Season to taste with salt and pepper; serve hot.

# TONKINESE SOUP

*Preparation time: 15 minutes*
*Cooking time: 10 minutes*
*4 servings*

| | | |
|---|---|---|
| 10 cups | chicken stock | 2.5 L |
| 3 tbsp | chopped fresh cilantro | 45 mL |
| 1 tbsp | fresh lime or lemon juice | 15 mL |
| 2 tsp | sesame oil | 10 mL |
| 3 | green onions, thinly sliced | 3 |
| 1 tsp | finely chopped fresh ginger | 5 mL |
| 4 oz | rice vermicelli noodles | 125 g |
| ½ lb | very thinly sliced chicken (fondue cut) | 250 g |
| | soy sauce | |
| | fresh bean sprouts | |
| | fresh cilantro | |

- In a large saucepan, bring stock to a boil. Add chopped cilantro, juice, sesame oil, green onions and ginger. Let simmer 2 to 3 minutes over medium heat.
- Add vermicelli noodles and cook until tender.
- Pour into large bowls and stir in sliced chicken (chicken will cook in hot stock).
- Serve at once with soy sauce, bean sprouts and cilantro for garnishing.

# CHICKEN TORTELLINI SOUP

*Preparation time: 10 minutes*
*Cooking time: 15 minutes*
*6 servings*

| | | |
|---|---|---|
| 2 tbsp | vegetable oil | 30 mL |
| 1 | small onion, chopped | 1 |
| 1 | celery stalk, diced | 1 |
| 1 | carrot, grated | 1 |
| 2 | garlic cloves, finely chopped | 2 |
| 1 tbsp | chopped fresh basil or 1 tsp (5 mL) dried basil | 15 mL |
| 3 cups | chicken stock | 750 mL |
| 1 cup | fresh cheese tortellini or ravioli | 250 mL |
| ¼ cup | shredded cabbage | 50 mL |
| 1 | can (28 oz/796 mL) diced tomatoes | 1 |
| 1 | can (19 oz/540 mL) kidney beans or chickpeas, drained | 1 |
| 1 cup | cubed cooked chicken | 250 mL |
| | salt and pepper | |

- Heat oil in a large saucepan. Add onion and sauté over medium heat 2 minutes.
- Add celery, carrot, garlic and basil. Cook 5 minutes. Add stock, tortellini, cabbage and tomatoes.
- Cover and simmer over low heat until tortellini is cooked as desired. Add kidney beans and chicken; simmer until heated through. Season to taste with salt and pepper; serve hot.

# CHICKEN
# VEGETABLE SOUP

*Preparation time: 15 minutes*
*Cooking time: 20 minutes*
*8 servings*

| | | |
|---|---|---|
| 1 tbsp | butter or oil | 15 mL |
| 1 | large onion, finely chopped | 1 |
| 2 tbsp | all-purpose flour | 30 mL |
| 4 cups | chicken stock | 1 L |
| 2 | potatoes, peeled and cubed | 2 |
| 2 | carrots, peeled and sliced | 2 |
| 2 | large celery stalks, thinly sliced | 2 |
| 1 tsp | poultry seasoning | 5 mL |
| 2 cups | cubed cooked chicken | 500 mL |
| 2 cups | 15% cream or evaporated milk | 500 mL |
| 10 oz | fresh or frozen chopped spinach | 300 g |
| ½ cup | chopped fresh parsley | 125 mL |
| | salt and pepper | |

■ Melt butter in a large saucepan. Add onion and cook over low heat until soft, but not browned. Sprinkle in flour and stir 1 to 2 minutes.

■ Add chicken stock, potatoes, carrots, celery and poultry seasoning. Season with salt and pepper.

■ Bring to a boil over high heat. Reduce heat to medium, cover, and cook 10 minutes.

■ Add chicken, cream, spinach and parsley. Lower heat and simmer 5 minutes or until heated through (do not let soup boil). Serve hot.

# CREAM OF CHICKEN
# AND MUSHROOM

**Preparation time: 15 minutes**
**Cooking time: 25 minutes**
**6 servings**

| | | |
|---|---|---|
| ¼ cup | butter or oil | 50 mL |
| 2 | onions, chopped | 2 |
| I cup | sliced mushrooms | 250 mL |
| ⅓ cup | all-purpose flour | 75 mL |
| 4 cups | chicken stock | I L |
| 2 cups | milk | 500 mL |
| 2 cups | diced cooked chicken | 500 mL |
| | salt and pepper | |
| | fresh chives | |

- Melt butter in a large saucepan over medium heat. Add onions and mushrooms; cook, stirring constantly, until vegetables are soft.

- Sprinkle in flour and cook, stirring constantly. Gradually stir in chicken stock and milk.

- Season to taste with salt and pepper. Bring to a boil, then cover and simmer 10 minutes over low heat.

- Add diced chicken and simmer until heated through. Purée in blender or food processor until smooth. Serve garnished with fresh chives.

# CHICKEN AND BARLEY SOUP

*Preparation time: 20 minutes*
*Cooking time: 35 minutes*
*4 servings*

| | | |
|---|---|---|
| 6 cups | chicken stock, skimmed | 1.5 L |
| 1 | carrot, peeled and diced | 1 |
| 1 | celery stalk, diced | 1 |
| 1 | small parsnip, peeled and diced | 1 |
| 1 | zucchini, diced | 1 |
| 2 | potatoes, peeled and diced | 2 |
| ⅓ cup | pearl barley | 75 mL |
| 2 | sprigs fresh thyme* | 2 |
| 2 | sprigs fresh oregano | 2 |
| 2 | sprigs fresh parsley | 2 |
| 1 | bay leaf | 1 |
| 2 cups | diced cooked chicken | 500 mL |
| | salt and pepper | |

- In a large saucepan, bring stock to a boil over medium heat. Add all vegetables and barley.
- Tie herbs and bay leaf together with kitchen string*. Add to stock. Season with salt and pepper.
- Simmer over low heat about 30 minutes, or until vegetables and barley are tender. Remove herb bundle. Add chicken and simmer until heated through.

*\* If you wish to use dried herbs, place 1 tsp (5 mL) each dried thyme, oregano and parsley along with bay leaf in small piece of cheesecloth or tea infuser.*

# CREAM OF CELERY AND APPLE

*Preparation time: 15 minutes*
*Cooking time: 40 minutes*
*6 servings*

| | | |
|---|---|---|
| 3 tbsp | butter or oil | 45 mL |
| 2 | leeks or onions, sliced | 2 |
| 4 | large apples, peeled, cored and chopped | 4 |
| 2 cups | diced celery | 500 mL |
| 2 | potatoes, peeled and diced | 2 |
| 6 cups | chicken stock | 1.5 L |
| ½ tsp | celery seeds | 2 mL |
| 2 | apples, unpeeled, cored and diced | 2 |
| | pinch ground nutmeg | |
| | salt and pepper | |

■ In a large saucepan, melt 2 tbsp (30 mL) butter over low heat. Add leeks, cover and cook about 5 minutes.

■ Add apples and celery. Cook, stirring constantly, 5 minutes. Add potatoes, chicken stock, celery seeds and nutmeg. Season with salt and pepper.

■ Bring to a boil. Cover, lower heat and simmer about 30 minutes. Puree in blender or food processor. Strain.

■ Sauté diced apples in remaining butter until golden. Sprinkle over hot soup.

*Sauté leeks in butter about 5 minutes.*

*Add apples and celery.*

Add potatoes, chicken
stock, celery seeds and
nutmeg.

Transfer to blender or food
processor.

Purée until smooth and
strain.

# SANDWICHES

With today's busy lifestyles, sandwiches can not only take the place of a whole meal, but can be served on all kinds of different occasions, including friendly lunches, brunches and picnics!

This chapter offers a variety of wholesome recipes for simple and delicious sandwiches that combine chicken with all kinds of fresh ingredients. From *Souvlaki Pita* to *Deviled Chicken Burgers*, these recipes are sure to become favorites among your family and friends.

# SOUVLAKI PITA

*Preparation time: 15 minutes*
*Marinating time: 30 minutes*
*Cooking time: 10 minutes*
*4 servings*

| | | |
|---|---|---|
| 2 tbsp | fresh lemon juice | 30 mL |
| 2 tbsp | olive oil | 30 mL |
| ½ tsp | salt | 2 mL |
| ½ tsp | pepper | 2 mL |
| ¼ tsp | ground cumin | I mL |
| ¼ tsp | dried oregano | I mL |
| 2 | garlic cloves, finely chopped | 2 |
| I lb | boneless, skinless chicken breasts or thighs, cubed | 500 g |
| 4 | pita breads | 4 |
| 2 | tomatoes, diced | 2 |

**Sauce:**

| | | |
|---|---|---|
| I tsp | salt | 5 mL |
| I | English cucumber, peeled, seeded and grated | I |
| ½ cup | plain yogurt | 125 mL |
| ½ cup | mayonnaise | 125 mL |
| 2 tbsp | chopped fresh mint | 30 mL |
| 2 tbsp | chopped fresh parsley | 30 mL |
| 2 | garlic cloves, finely chopped | 2 |
| | dash Tabasco sauce | |

- In a medium bowl, stir together lemon juice, olive oil, salt, pepper, cumin, oregano and garlic. Place chicken in mixture; stir to coat on all sides. Cover and refrigerate at least 30 minutes.

- Meanwhile, sprinkle 1 tsp (5 mL) salt over grated cucumber and mix well. Place cucumber in a strainer and let drain 15 minutes. Pat gently with paper towels to remove excess liquid.

- Place cucumber in bowl with remaining sauce ingredients. Mix well.

- Thread marinated chicken onto 4 skewers. Cook on barbecue over medium-high heat about 5 minutes on each side, or until cooked through.

- Remove chicken from skewers and place on pita breads. Top generously with tomatoes and cucumber sauce. Roll up and serve hot.

# HERBED CHICKEN
# ON RYE

**Preparation time: 10 minutes**
**6 servings**

| | | |
|---|---|---|
| ½ cup | mayonnaise | 125 mL |
| 1 tbsp | Meaux or Dijon mustard | 15 mL |
| 1 | green onion, chopped | 1 |
| 2 tbsp | chopped fresh chives | 30 mL |
| 2 tbsp | chopped fresh parsley | 30 mL |
| ½ tsp | salt | 2 mL |
| ½ tsp | pepper | 2 mL |
| 12 | slices of rye bread, toasted | 12 |
| ½ | English cucumber, thinly sliced | ½ |
| 3 | boneless, skinless chicken breasts, cooked and sliced | 3 |
| ½ lb | Cheddar cheese, sliced | 250 g |
| 6 | Boston lettuce leaves | 6 |

■ In a bowl, stir together mayonnaise, mustard, onion, chives, parsley, salt and pepper.

■ Spread herb mixture over bread slices. Cover each of 6 slices with cucumber and chicken; top with cheese and lettuce. Cover with another slice of rye and serve immediately.

# DEVILED CHICKEN BURGERS

*Preparation time: 10 minutes*
*Cooking time: 10 minutes*
*4 servings*

| | | |
|---|---|---:|
| ⅓ cup | quick-cooking couscous | 75 mL |
| ½ cup | boiling water | 125 mL |
| 2 tsp | vegetable oil | 10 mL |
| I | hot red chili pepper, minced (optional) | I |
| I tsp | dried thyme | 5 mL |
| I tsp | curry powder | 5 mL |
| ½ tsp | *each* ground cumin, ginger and allspice | 2 mL |
| ½ tsp | salt | 2 mL |
| ¼ tsp | pepper | I mL |
| ¼ tsp | paprika | I mL |
| ⅛ tsp | cayenne pepper | 0.5 mL |
| 2 | garlic cloves, finely chopped | 2 |
| I lb | ground chicken | 500 g |
| 4 | kaiser rolls or hamburger buns | 4 |
| 4 | tomato slices | 4 |
| ¾ cup | grated Mozzarella cheese | 175 mL |
| 4 | lettuce leaves, shredded | 4 |

- Preheat barbecue to medium. Place couscous in a small bowl. Pour in boiling water and stir with a fork. Cover with plastic wrap and let stand 5 minutes.
- Heat oil in a skillet over medium heat. Add chili pepper and all seasonings. Stir-fry 2 minutes. Let cool.
- In a medium bowl, place couscous, spice mixture, garlic, and chicken. Mix well. Shape chicken mixture into 4 patties. Grill on barbecue 3 to 4 minutes each side.
- Place one tomato slice on bottom of each kaiser roll. Place burgers over tomatoes; top with Mozzarella cheese, lettuce and top halves of rolls.

**Note:** *Burgers can also be cooked in a skillet or grilled in the oven.*

## CHICKEN PITA POCKETS
## WITH CELERY ROOT

**Preparation time: 10 minutes**
**6 servings**

| | | |
|---|---|---|
| 2 tbsp | sour cream | 30 mL |
| ¼ cup | mayonnaise | 50 mL |
| 2 tbsp | chopped fresh tarragon | 30 mL |
| ½ tsp | mustard seeds | 2 mL |
| 1½ cups | peeled, grated celery root (celeriac) | 375 mL |
| 3 cups | diced cooked chicken | 750 mL |
| 6 | pita breads | 6 |
| 6 | lettuce leaves | 6 |
| | Tabasco sauce | |
| | salt and pepper | |

- In a bowl, stir together sour cream, mayonnaise, tarragon and a few drops Tabasco sauce. Season with salt and pepper.
- Stir in mustard seeds, celery root and chicken. Mix well.
- Cut pita breads in 2. Open and stuff each half with lettuce and chicken mixture.

# OPEN-FACED BREADED CHICKEN SANDWICHES

*Preparation time: 20 minutes*
*Chilling time: 30 minutes*
*Cooking time: 10 minutes*
*4 servings*

| | | |
|---|---|---|
| 4 | boneless, skinless chicken breast halves (1lb/500 g) | 4 |
| 1 | egg | 1 |
| 2 tbsp | water | 30 mL |
| ¾ cup | dry breadcrumbs | 175 mL |
| 2 tbsp | grated Parmesan cheese | 30 mL |
| ½ tsp | paprika | 2 mL |
| 4 | thick slices of farmhouse bread | 4 |
| 2 | tomatoes, sliced | 2 |
| ¼ cup | bottled marinated eggplant, chopped | 50 mL |
| | extra virgin olive oil | |
| | grated Parmesan cheese | |
| | pepper | |

- Oil and preheat barbecue or oven grill to medium-high heat.
- Place chicken between 2 sheets of waxed paper and pound gently to flatten.
- Beat egg and water together in a shallow bowl. In a second shallow bowl, stir together breadcrumbs, cheese, paprika and pepper to taste.
- Dip chicken on both sides in egg mixture, then in crumbs. Arrange in single layer on a plate and cover with waxed paper. Refrigerate about 30 minutes.
- Grill chicken 5 inches (12 cm) from heat, 4 to 5 minutes on each side, or until no longer pink inside.
- Brush each slice of bread with olive oil and grill. Divide tomato slices and chicken breast halves between slices of bread. Sprinkle with chopped eggplant and Parmesan cheese. Serve hot.

# CHICKEN AND
# RED PEPPER FOCACCIA

*Preparation time: 20 minutes*
*Marinating time: 30 minutes*
*Cooking time: 15 minutes*
*4 servings*

| | | |
|---|---|---|
| 2 | boneless, skinless chicken breast halves (½ lb/250 g) | 2 |
| ⅓ cup | olive oil | 75 mL |
| 2 tbsp | fresh lemon juice | 30 mL |
| I tbsp | white wine vinegar | 15 mL |
| I tbsp | finely chopped fresh basil or I tsp (5 mL) dried basil | 15 mL |
| I | garlic clove, finely chopped | I |
| ½ tsp | Dijon mustard | 2 mL |
| ½ tsp | granulated sugar | 2 mL |
| 2 | red bell peppers | 2 |
| I | focaccia 16 x 12 inches (40 x 30 cm) | I |
| | freshly ground black pepper | |
| | fresh basil leaves | |

- Preheat barbecue to medium-high heat. Place chicken in a large, sealable plastic bag.

- In a bowl, stir together oil, lemon juice, vinegar, basil, garlic, mustard, sugar and black pepper to taste. Pour ½ the mixture over chicken and set remaining mixture aside for basting. Seal plastic bag, pressing out excess air, and refrigerate at least 30 minutes.

- Meanwhile, grill whole red peppers on barbecue until skin is blackened on all sides. Place peppers in paper bag, fold shut, and let cool 10 minutes.

- Pull skins from peppers. Cut peppers in 4; discard seeds and membranes. Set aside.

- Drain chicken, discarding marinade. Place chicken pieces on oiled barbecue rack about 5 inches (12 cm) from coals. Cook about 7 minutes on each side, or until no longer pink inside. Baste with reserved oil mixture during first half of cooking. Let cool slightly and slice.

- Cut foccacia in 4, then cut each piece in half along the thickness. Distribute chicken, grilled peppers and basil among 4 pieces. Top with remaining pieces of focaccia and serve.

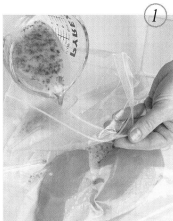

*Pour oil mixture over chicken in plastic bag. Seal and refrigerate at least 30 minutes.*

*Cut foccacia in 4, then cut each piece in half along the thickness.*

*Distribute chicken, grilled peppers and basil among 4 pieces. Top with remaining pieces.*

# BLUE CHEESE AND
# CHICKEN SANDWICHES

*Preparation time: 10 minutes*
*Cooking time: 10 minutes*
*4 servings*

| | | |
|---|---|---|
| 1 lb | ground chicken | 500 g |
| ½ cup | dry breadcrumbs | 125 mL |
| 2 | eggs, beaten | 2 |
| 2 tbsp | chili sauce | 30 mL |
| 2 tbsp | dried parsley | 30 mL |
| 1 | onion, finely chopped | 1 |
| ½ tsp | cayenne pepper | 2 mL |
| 8 | slices of pumpernickel bread | 8 |
| 2 | tomatoes, sliced | 2 |
| 1 cup | chopped spinach | 250 mL |

**Blue Cheese Sauce:**

| | | |
|---|---|---|
| ¾ cup | mayonnaise | 175 mL |
| 1 | green onion, chopped | 1 |
| 1 | garlic clove, chopped | 1 |
| ¼ tsp | black pepper | 1 mL |
| 2 tbsp | skim milk | 30 mL |
| 3½ oz | blue cheese | 100 g |

- In a medium bowl, combine chicken, breadcrumbs, eggs, chili sauce, parsley, onion and cayenne pepper. Shape into 4 flat patties.

- Arrange patties on a well-greased baking sheet. Broil about 6 inches (15 cm) from heat, 5 minutes on each side.

- Meanwhile, in a blender or food processor, combine all sauce ingredients and process until almost smooth; set aside.

- Divide tomato slices between 4 slices of bread. Place chicken patties over tomatoes; top with blue cheese sauce, spinach and remaining slices of bread.

## SESAME CHICKEN BAGUETTES

**Preparation time: 10 minutes**
**6 servings**

| | | |
|---|---|---|
| 6 | small baguettes or long rolls | 6 |
| 2 tbsp | red wine vinegar | 30 mL |
| 1 tsp | sesame oil or vegetable oil | 5 mL |
| 2 tsp | fresh lemon juice | 10 mL |
| 3 tbsp | mayonnaise | 45 mL |
| 3 cups | diced cooked chicken | 750 mL |
| ⅓ cup | chopped green onions | 75 mL |
| ½ tsp | sesame seeds | 2 mL |
| | Tabasco sauce | |
| | salt and pepper | |
| | snow pea sprouts or alfalfa sprouts | |

- Slice baguettes open lengthwise.
- In a bowl, blend vinegar, oil, lemon juice and mayonnaise. Add chicken, green onion, a few drops of Tabasco sauce, and sesame seeds. Season with salt and pepper. Mix well.
- Divide mixture evenly over bottom halves of baguettes. Top with sprouts and serve.

## GRILLED CHICKEN
## AND PESTO PANINI

**Preparation time: 5 minutes**
**Marinating time: 1 hour**
**Cooking time: 10 minutes**
**2 servings**

| | | |
|---|---|---|
| 2 | boneless, skinless chicken breast halves (½ lb/250 g) | 2 |
| 1 cup | basil pesto (see recipe p. 167) | 250 mL |
| 2 | ciabattas or 1 baguette, cut in half | 2 |
| 10 | sun-dried tomatoes in oil, drained | 10 |
| 4 | slices Provolone cheese | 4 |
| | curly endive leaves | |

- Marinate chicken in ¾ cup (175 mL) pesto sauce 1 hour.

- Heat barbecue to medium. Discard pesto marinade and cook chicken on oiled grill 3 to 4 minutes each side, or until no longer pink inside.

- Slice ciabattas open lengthwise. Brush inside with remaining ¼ cup (50 mL) pesto sauce and line bottom halves with sun-dried tomatoes. Slice chicken and layer over tomatoes. Top with cheese and curly endive leaves.

- Close sandwiches and grill on barbecue 2 minutes on each side, pressing down on them to melt the cheese.

**Tip:** You can also cook the chicken and/or grill the whole sandwich in a skillet.

# BAGELS WITH LEMON CHICKEN AND AVOCADO SAUCE

**Preparation time: 10 minutes**
**Cooking time: 5 minutes**
**4 servings**

| | | |
|---|---|---|
| 1 lb | ground chicken | 500 g |
| 1 | egg | 1 |
| ½ cup | dry breadcrumbs | 125 mL |
| 1 tsp | salt | 5 mL |
| ½ tsp | pepper | 2 mL |
| ½ tsp | dried oregano | 2 mL |
| ½ tsp | paprika | 2 mL |
| ½ tsp | grated lemon zest | 2 mL |
| 1 | garlic clove, finely chopped | 1 |
| 4 | bagels, sliced in half | 4 |
| 2 | tomatoes, sliced | 2 |
| 1 cup | sliced fresh mushrooms | 250 mL |
| | Romaine lettuce | |

## Avocado Sauce:

| | | |
|---|---|---|
| ¼ lb | cream cheese | 125 g |
| 2 | ripe avocados, peeled and pitted | 2 |
| 1 | garlic clove, finely chopped | 1 |
| ½ cup | plain yogurt | 125 mL |
| ½ tsp | Tabasco sauce (optional) | 2 mL |
| | juice of ½ lemon | |

- Preheat barbecue to medium.
- Combine chicken, egg, breadcrumbs, salt, pepper, oregano, paprika, lemon zest and garlic. Shape into 4 patties about 4 inches (10 cm) in diameter and ¾-inch (2 cm) thick.
- Cook on oiled barbecue grill 5 minutes, or until no longer pink inside.
- Meanwhile, with an electric mixer, combine all sauce ingredients.
- Arrange tomato slices then sliced mushrooms over bottom half of each bagel. Place chicken on top and cover with avocado sauce, lettuce and top halves of bagels.

# EASY EVERYDAY DISHES

**T**he best meals are often the easiest to prepare. In this chapter, you'll discover a whole range of exciting new dishes that don't require much planning or slaving over a hot stove.

*Chicken Enchiladas, Ginger Chicken with Maple Syrup, Chicken Portobello Pasta…* these are just some of the delicious dishes you can serve any day of the week, when you want to treat yourself and your family!

# ASIAN-STYLE
# GLAZED CHICKEN

*Preparation time: 15 minutes*
*Cooking time: 20 minutes*
*4 servings*

| | | |
|---|---|---|
| ½ cup | rice vinegar or dry sherry | 125 mL |
| ½ cup | orange or pineapple juice | 125 mL |
| 2 tbsp | soy sauce | 30 mL |
| 2 tbsp | honey | 30 mL |
| ½ tsp | *each* ground cinnamon, ginger, salt and pepper | 2 mL |
| 8 | chicken thighs | 8 |
| 1 tbsp | peanut oil | 15 mL |
| 1 | garlic clove, finely chopped | 1 |
| 1 | hot red chili pepper, minced (optional) | 1 |
| 1 tsp | cornstarch dissolved in 1 tbsp (15 mL) water | 5 mL |
| 2 | green onions, chopped | 2 |
| | rice vermicelli noodles, cooked | |

■ In measuring cup or small bowl, stir together rice vinegar, juice, soy sauce and honey; set aside.

■ In another small bowl, stir together cinnamon, ginger, salt and pepper. Roll chicken thighs in spice mixture.

■ Heat oil in large skillet over high heat. Add chicken and stir-fry quickly to brown all sides. Reduce heat to medium and continue cooking 12 to 15 minutes, until chicken is no longer pink inside. Remove chicken from skillet and set aside along with cooking liquid.

■ Increase heat to medium-high and stir in vinegar mixture. Bring to a boil, and cook 2 to 3 minutes until reduced by half.

■ Reduce heat to low. Stir in garlic, hot pepper and reserved chicken with liquid. Stir until chicken is heated through and coated with sauce.

■ Transfer chicken to individual plates. Add cornstarch mixture to pan juices and stir until smooth. Pour over chicken and garnish with green onions. Serve at once with vermicelli and steamed vegetables, if desired.

## BREADED CHICKEN ROLLS
## WITH HAM AND CHEESE

*Preparation time: 10 minutes*
*Cooking time: 15 minutes*
*4 servings*

| | | |
|---|---|---|
| 4 | boneless, skinless chicken breast halves (1 lb/500g) | 4 |
| 4 | slices smoked Black Forest ham | 4 |
| 4 | slices Gruyère cheese | 4 |
| 4 | fresh basil leaves | 4 |
| ¼ cup | all-purpose flour | 50 mL |
| 1 | egg, beaten | 1 |
| ½ cup | dry breadcrumbs | 125 mL |
| 1 tbsp | vegetable oil | 15 mL |

■ Preheat oven to 350°F (180°C).

■ Make long deep slit on side of each chicken breast with a sharp knife to make a pocket. Place 1 slice of ham, 1 slice of cheese and 1 basil leaf in each pocket.

■ Roll chicken pockets and hold closed with toothpicks. Coat both sides with flour. Dip in beaten egg, then coat in breadcrumbs.

■ Heat oil in skillet over medium-high heat. Brown chicken on both sides.

■ Arrange chicken in baking pan and bake 10 to 12 minutes, depending on thickness, until chicken is no longer pink inside.

■ Slice chicken rolls crosswise and serve with vegetables and noodles, if desired.

# GINGER CHICKEN
# WITH MAPLE SYRUP

*Preparation time: 15 minutes*
*Cooking time: 10 minutes*
*4 to 6 servings*

| | | |
|---|---|---|
| 2 tsp | vegetable oil | 10 mL |
| 1¼ lbs | boneless, skinless chicken thighs, cut in strips | 625 g |
| ⅓ cup | all-purpose flour | 75 mL |
| ½ cup | maple syrup | 125 mL |
| 2 tbsp | cider vinegar | 30 mL |
| 2 tbsp | soy sauce | 30 mL |
| 2 tbsp | dry sherry (optional) | 30 mL |
| 2 tsp | grated fresh ginger | 10 mL |
| 2 | garlic cloves, finely chopped | 2 |
| ½ tsp | pepper | 2 mL |

- Preheat oven to 325°F (160°C). Heat oil in an ovenproof casserole or baking dish over medium heat. Roll chicken strips in flour and cook, stirring occasionally, about 5 minutes, or until browned on all sides.

- Stir together syrup, vinegar, soy sauce, sherry, ginger, garlic and pepper. Pour over chicken.

- Bake in oven 5 to 10 minutes, depending on size of chicken pieces, until juices run clear when pierced with a fork. Serve with mashed sweet potatoes and green beans, if desired.

# THREE-CHEESE
# CHICKEN LASAGNA

*Preparation time: 20 minutes*
*Cooking time: 1 hour*
*8 servings*

## Meat Sauce:

| | | |
|---|---|---|
| 1 lb | ground chicken | 500 g |
| 2 | onions, chopped | 2 |
| 2 | garlic cloves, finely chopped | 2 |
| 2 tsp | *each* dried basil, oregano and salt | 10 mL |
| 1½ cups | sliced fresh mushrooms | 375 mL |
| 1 | can (5½ oz/156 mL) tomato paste | 1 |
| 1 | can (19 oz/540 mL) tomato sauce | 1 |
| 1 cup | water | 250 mL |
| 1 tsp | sugar | 5 mL |
| | pinch pepper | |

## Lasagna:

| | | |
|---|---|---|
| 1 lb | cottage cheese | 500 g |
| 2 | eggs, beaten | 2 |
| ½ cup | grated Parmesan cheese | 125 mL |
| ½ lb | sliced Mozzarella cheese | 250 g |
| 9 | oven-ready lasagna noodles | 9 |

- In large nonstick skillet over medium-high heat, stir-fry chicken, onion, garlic, basil, oregano and salt until chicken is no longer pink. Add remaining sauce ingredients and simmer 30 minutes.

- Preheat oven to 350°F (180°C). Mix cottage cheese, beaten eggs and Parmesan.

- Spread ¼ of the meat sauce in bottom of 9 x 13-inch (22 x 33 cm) pan. Top with 3 noodles. Top with ¼ of sauce, ½ of cottage cheese mixture and ⅓ of Mozzarella cheese.

- Repeat layers. Finish with 3 noodles, remaining sauce and Mozzarella cheese. Bake 30 minutes, or until noodles are tender and cheese has melted.

# ORANGE AND ALMOND
# CHICKEN STIR-FRY

*Preparation time: 15 minutes*
*Cooking time: 12 minutes*
*4 servings*

| | | |
|---|---|---|
| 1 tsp | cornstarch | 5 mL |
| ½ cup | orange juice | 125 mL |
| 2 tbsp | vegetable oil | 30 mL |
| 1 lb | boneless, skinless chicken breast, cut in strips | 500 g |
| 1 | onion, halved and thinly sliced | 1 |
| 2 | carrots, thinly sliced | 2 |
| 1 | celery stalk, thinly sliced | 1 |
| 1 cup | broccoli florets | 250 mL |
| ¼ cup | chicken stock | 50 mL |
| 1 tbsp | grated orange zest | 15 mL |
| ½ tsp | salt | 2 mL |
| ½ tsp | pepper | 2 mL |
| 2 tbsp | toasted almonds | 30 mL |
| | steamed rice | |

■ Dissolve cornstarch in orange juice. Set aside.

■ Heat oil in large skillet or wok. Add chicken and stir-fry over medium-high heat 5 minutes. Remove chicken and set aside.

■ Add onion, carrots and celery to skillet. Stir-fry 2 minutes. Add broccoli and chicken stock. Cover and cook 3 to 4 minutes, or until vegetables are tender but still crisp.

■ Return chicken to skillet. Add orange juice mixture, zest, salt and pepper. Cook about 1 minute, until sauce thickens.

■ Serve hot over steamed rice and sprinkle with toasted almonds.

*1*

*Heat oil in large skillet or wok. Add chicken and stir-fry over medium-high heat 5 minutes.*

*2*

*Add onion, carrots and celery to skillet. Stir-fry 2 minutes.*

*3*

*Add broccoli and chicken stock. Cover and cook 3 to 4 minutes.*

# CRISPY BAKED
# CHICKEN SCHNITZEL

*Preparation time: 5 minutes*
*Cooking time: 20 minutes*
*4 servings*

| | | |
|---|---|---|
| 4 | boneless, skinless chicken breast halves (1 lb/500 g) | 4 |
| ½ cup | all-purpose flour | 125 mL |
| 2 | eggs, beaten | 2 |
| 2½ cups | crushed corn flakes | 625 mL |
| 1 tsp | vegetable oil | 5 mL |
| | salt and pepper | |

- Preheat oven to 400°F (200°C).
- Season chicken with salt and pepper. Coat with flour then dip in beaten egg. Coat with corn flakes.
- Place chicken on oiled baking sheet and bake 20 minutes or until chicken is no longer pink inside.
- Serve with mashed potatoes and vegetables, if desired.

## CHICKEN PORTOBELLO
## PASTA

*Preparation time: 15 minutes*
*Cooking time: 15 minutes*
*4 servings*

| | | |
|---|---|---|
| 1 tbsp | olive oil | 15 mL |
| 1 lb | boneless, skinless chicken breast, cut in strips | 500 g |
| 4 | shallots, chopped | 4 |
| 1 | portobello mushroom, chopped | 1 |
| 1 cup | snow peas | 250 mL |
| ⅓ cup | dry white wine | 75 mL |
| ½ cup | heavy cream (35%) | 125 mL |
| ½ tsp | dried thyme | 2 mL |
| ½ tsp | salt | 2 mL |
| ¼ tsp | pepper | 1 mL |
| 4 | sun-dried tomatoes in oil, drained and chopped | 4 |
| 2 cups | penne pasta | 500 mL |
| | grated Parmesan cheese | |

■ Heat oil in a large skillet over medium heat. Add chicken strips and stir-fry 5 minutes.

■ Stir in shallots, mushroom and snow peas. Continue cooking 3 to 4 minutes or until chicken is no longer pink inside. Stir in wine and cook 2 minutes.

■ Add cream, seasonings and tomato. Cook over low heat until sauce is slightly thickened. Keep warm.

■ Cook pasta in boiling salted water. Drain and toss with sauce. Serve immediately, with grated Parmesan cheese.

# CHICKEN AND
# PORK PIE

*Preparation time: 15 minutes*
*Cooking time: 30 minutes*
*6 servings*

| | | |
|---|---|---|
| 1 tbsp | butter | 15 mL |
| 1 | medium onion, chopped | 1 |
| ½ lb | ground chicken | 250 g |
| ½ lb | ground pork | 250 g |
| 1 tsp | salt | 5 mL |
| ½ tsp | pepper | 2 mL |
| ¼ tsp | ground cloves | 1 mL |
| ¼ tsp | ground nutmeg | 1 mL |
| ⅓ cup | chicken stock | 75 mL |
| 1 | egg, beaten | 1 |
| | pastry for 8-inch (20 cm) double crust pie | |

- Preheat oven to 400°F (200°C).
- Melt butter in a large saucepan; add onion and cook over medium heat until soft. Add chicken, pork, salt and pepper; cook 6 to 8 minutes, or until no longer pink.
- Add clove, nutmeg and chicken stock; continue cooking until liquid has evaporated. Remove from heat.
- Line an 8-inch (20 cm) pie plate with pastry. Brush edges with beaten egg.
- Drain fat from chicken mixture and place in pie shell. Cover with second pastry layer and seal edges.
- With sharp knife, cut slit in top crust and brush with beaten egg. Bake 20 to 25 minutes, or until crust is golden brown.
- Serve with steamed vegetables and tomato relish, if desired.

# SUPER SPAGHETTI SAUCE

*Preparation time: 25 minutes*
*Cooking time: 2½ hours*
*12 servings*

| | | |
|---|---|---|
| I tbsp | vegetable oil | 15 mL |
| 4 | onions, finely chopped | 4 |
| 2 | *each* celery stalks, carrots and bell peppers, diced | 2 |
| I lb | mushrooms, sliced | 500 g |
| 2 lbs | ground chicken | I kg |
| 3 | garlic cloves, finely chopped | 3 |
| I | can (48 oz/1.36 L) tomato juice | I |
| 2 | cans (19 oz / 540 mL *each*) diced Italian tomatoes | 2 |
| I | can (5½ oz/156 mL) tomato paste | I |
| I | package (10 oz/300 g) fresh spinach, cleaned and chopped | I |
| ½ tsp | *each* dried thyme, oregano, marjoram and red pepper flakes | 2 mL |
| I tbsp | dried basil | 15 mL |
| 2 | bay leaves | 2 |
| I tbsp | sugar | 15 mL |
| | salt and pepper to taste | |

- Heat oil in large saucepan. Add vegetables and cook over medium heat, stirring occasionally, until softened.
- Add chicken. Cook, stirring constantly, 7 or 8 minutes.
- Add remaining ingredients. Cook over low heat 2 to 2½ hours, stirring occasionally.

**Tip:** This sauce freezes well in individual or family-size containers.

# PRESTO CHICKEN
# WITH BECHAMEL SAUCE

*Preparation time: 10 minutes*
*Cooking time: 20 minutes*
*4 servings*

| | | |
|---|---|---|
| 2½ cups | tri-color wagon wheel pasta | 625 mL |
| 3 cups | cubed cooked chicken | 750 mL |
| 2½ cups | bechamel sauce (see recipe p.166) | 625 mL |
| 2 tbsp | chopped fresh parsley | 30 mL |
| ¼ cup | dry breadcrumbs | 50 mL |
| ½ cup | grated Parmesan cheese salt and pepper | 125 mL |

- Preheat oven to 400°F (200°C). Cook pasta in boiling, salted water; drain well and set aside.

- Meanwhile, in large saucepan, mix together chicken and bechamel sauce. Stir over low heat until heated through. Add parsley; season with salt and pepper. Set aside.

- Grease 4 individual, oven-proof dishes or a 9-inch (23 cm) square baking dish. Line dishes with pasta. Top with chicken mixture. Sprinkle with breadcrumbs and Parmesan cheese.

- Bake about 20 minutes, until golden and bubbly.

# CHICKEN
# TETRAZZINI

*Preparation time: 15 minutes*
*Cooking time: 15 minutes*
*4 servings*

| | | |
|---|---|---|
| 2 tsp | butter | 10 mL |
| 2 tsp | olive oil | 10 mL |
| 1 | medium onion, chopped | 1 |
| ¾ cup | sliced mushrooms | 175 mL |
| ⅓ cup | sliced celery | 75 mL |
| 1 | garlic clove, finely chopped | 1 |
| 2 tbsp | all-purpose flour | 30 mL |
| 1½ cups | milk | 375 mL |
| 1½ cups | chicken stock | 375 mL |
| ½ cup | grated Gruyère cheese | 125 mL |
| 1 tsp | chopped fresh tarragon or ½ tsp (2 mL) dried | 5 mL |
| 1½ cups | cubed cooked chicken | 375 mL |
| | salt and pepper | |
| | cooked linguine | |

- In a skillet, heat butter and oil over medium-high heat. Add onion, mushrooms, celery and garlic. Cook, stirring constantly, 2 to 3 minutes, until vegetables are soft. Stir in flour.

- Add milk and chicken stock. Cook over medium heat 4 to 5 minutes, or until sauce is smooth and creamy.

- Add half the grated cheese. Continue cooking until cheese melts. Add tarragon; season with salt and pepper. Add chicken and cook 2 to 3 minutes, until heated through.

- Serve sauce over hot cooked linguine, garnished with remaining cheese.

## SPICY THAI CHICKEN
## WITH BASIL

*Preparation time: 10 minutes*
*Cooking time: 45 minutes*
*4 servings*

| | | |
|---|---|---|
| 2 tbsp | vegetable oil | 30 mL |
| 1¼ lbs | chicken drumsticks | 625 g |
| 2 tbsp | chicken stock | 30 mL |
| 2 tbsp | oyster sauce or hoisin sauce* | 30 mL |
| 2 tbsp | nam pla fish sauce* | 30 mL |
| ¼ tsp | salt | 1 mL |
| 1 tsp | hot chili pepper flakes | 5 mL |
| ⅛ tsp | paprika | 0.5 mL |
| 8 to 12 | fresh basil leaves | 8 to 12 |
| 1 | green bell pepper, cut in strips | 1 |
| 1 | red bell pepper, cut in strips | 1 |
| | steamed rice | |

■ Preheat oven to 375°F (190°C). Heat oil in large skillet over high heat. Stir-fry chicken about 5 minutes.

■ Add chicken stock, oyster sauce, fish sauce, salt, red pepper flakes and paprika. Stir-fry 2 to 3 minutes. Spoon into baking dish. Cover and bake 30 minutes.

■ Add basil and bell peppers; continue baking, uncovered, 5 minutes. Serve with steamed rice, if desired.

*Available in Asian specialty food stores and gourmet supermarkets. You can also use nuoc mam sauce or soy sauce instead of nam pla sauce.

# CHICKEN AND VEGETABLE PIE

*Preparation time: 15 minutes*
*Cooking time: 45 minutes*
*6 servings*

| | | |
|---|---|---|
| 1 cup | chicken stock | 250 mL |
| ⅓ cup | green beans, cut in short lengths | 75 mL |
| ½ cup | diced carrots | 125 mL |
| 1 | medium onion, coarsely chopped | 1 |
| 1 tbsp | butter | 15 mL |
| 1 tbsp | all-purpose flour | 15 mL |
| 1 | can (10 oz/284 mL) condensed cream of mushroom soup | 1 |
| 2 tbsp | chopped fresh basil or 2 tsp (10 mL) dried basil | 30 mL |
| ⅓ cup | frozen or canned peas | 75 mL |
| 3 cups | cubed cooked chicken | 750 mL |
| 1 | egg, beaten | 1 |
| | salt and pepper | |
| | pastry for 8-inch (20 cm) double crust pie | |

■ Preheat oven to 375°F (190°C). In large saucepan, bring stock to a boil. Add beans, carrots and onion. Cook 5 to 6 minutes.

■ Meanwhile, in a second saucepan, melt butter over medium-low heat. Stir in flour until smooth. Let cool.

■ With a slotted spoon, remove vegetables from stock and set aside. Gradually pour stock into flour mixture, whisking vigorously. Cook over medium heat 4 to 5 minutes, until sauce is smooth and creamy.

■ Add mushroom soup and basil. Add reserved vegetables, peas and chicken. Season to taste with salt and pepper. Let mixture cool slightly.

■ Line an 8-inch (20 cm) pie plate with pastry. Brush edges with egg. Fill with chicken mixture. Top with second pastry layer and seal edges. With sharp knife, trim excess pastry along the edge. Cut slit in top crust and brush with beaten egg.

■ Bake 30 to 35 minutes, or until crust is golden brown.

*1*

Bring stock to a boil. Add beans, carrots and onion. Cook 5 to 6 minutes.

*2*

Gradually pour stock into flour mixture, whisking vigorously.

*3*

Add mushroom soup and basil.

Add reserved vegetables, peas and chicken.

Fill pie pastry with chicken mixture.

Top with second pastry layer and seal edges. Trim excess pastry along the edge.

# CHICKEN
# ENCHILADAS

*Preparation time: 10 minutes*
*Cooking time: 20 minutes*
*4 servings*

| | | |
|---|---|---|
| 2 cups | diced cooked chicken | 500 mL |
| ½ cup | finely chopped onion | 125 mL |
| I cup | grated Monterey Jack or Brick cheese | 250 mL |
| 3 tbsp | grated Parmesan cheese | 45 mL |
| I tsp | *each* salt, pepper and ground cumin | 5 mL |
| I tbsp | Worcestershire sauce | 15 mL |
| I | garlic clove, finely chopped | I |
| I | hot red chili pepper, minced (optional) | I |
| 2 tbsp | chopped fresh cilantro | 30 mL |
| 8 | 8-inch (20 cm) flour tortillas | 8 |
| I cup | salsa | 250 mL |
| I cup | grated Monterey Jack or Brick cheese | 250 mL |
| ½ cup | sour cream (optional) | 125 mL |
| ¼ cup | guacamole (optional) | 50 mL |

■ Preheat oven to 350°F (180°C). In a bowl, stir together the first 11 ingredients. Divide mixture among tortillas, placing it near edge.

■ Roll tortillas to enclose filling. Spread ⅓ cup (75 ml) salsa in bottom of baking pan. Arrange rolled tortillas side by side over salsa. Top with remaining salsa.

■ Sprinkle cheese over tortillas. Bake 20 minutes. Brown under broiler 2 minutes, if desired. Serve garnished with sour cream and guacamole, if desired.

## CHICKEN STROGANOFF

*Preparation time: 15 minutes*
*Cooking time: 15 minutes*
*6 servings*

| | | |
|---|---|---|
| 2 tsp | butter | 10 mL |
| 2 tsp | olive oil | 10 mL |
| 1 ½ lbs | boneless, skinless chicken breast, cut in strips | 750 g |
| ½ cup | chopped onion | 125 mL |
| ½ cup | quartered mushrooms | 125 mL |
| 3 tbsp | paprika | 45 mL |
| 1 tbsp | chopped fresh thyme or ½ tsp (2 mL) dried thyme | 15 mL |
| ¼ cup | dry white wine | 50 mL |
| ¾ cup | chicken stock | 175 mL |
| ½ cup | sour cream | 125 mL |
| ¼ cup | chopped fresh chives | 50 mL |
| | salt and pepper | |

■ Heat butter and oil in large skillet. Add chicken and cook 6 to 8 minutes over medium-high heat until chicken is no longer pink. Season with salt and pepper.

■ Add onions and mushrooms. Cook 3 to 4 minutes until soft. Sprinkle with paprika and thyme.

■ Add white wine and stir. Add stock. Bring to a boil and cook 3 to 4 minutes. Lower heat and stir in sour cream. Garnish with chives and serve with hot cooked noodles, if desired.

# CHICKEN PASTA SAUTÉ
## WITH WHITL WINE SAUCE

*Preparation time: 15 minutes*
*Cooking time: 25 minutes*
*6 servings*

## White Wine Sauce:

| 2 tbsp | olive oil | 30 mL |
|---|---|---|
| 2 tbsp | finely chopped shallots | 30 mL |
| 2 tbsp | finely chopped garlic | 30 mL |
| 1 cup | dry white wine | 250 mL |
| 1 | can crushed tomatoes (28 oz/796 mL) | 1 |
| 1½ cups | chicken stock | 375 mL |
| 1 tsp | *each* dried oregano and basil | 5 mL |
| 1 | bouquet garni* | 1 |
| 1 tbsp | cornstarch dissolved in water | 15 mL |
| ½ cup | table cream (15%) salt and pepper | 125 mL |

## Pasta:

| 3 cups | gemelli or farfalle pasta | 750 mL |
|---|---|---|
| 1 tbsp | olive oil | 15 mL |
| 1 lb | boneless, skinless chicken breast, cut in strips | 500 g |
| ½ | red bell pepper, sliced | ½ |
| ¾ cup | chopped fresh basil salt and pepper | 175 mL |

- Heat 2 tbsp (30 mL) oil in a saucepan over medium heat. Add shallots and garlic; cook 3 minutes.
- Add wine, tomatoes, chicken stock, oregano, dried basil and bouquet garni; season with salt and pepper. Cover and let simmer about 25 minutes over low heat.
- Meanwhile, cook pasta in boiling salted water.
- While pasta is cooking, heat oil in a large skillet over medium-high heat. Add chicken and stir-fry 5 minutes. Season with salt and pepper. Add red pepper. Cook over low heat 2 minutes. Add fresh basil and remove from heat.
- Remove bouquet garni from white wine sauce; stir in dissolved cornstarch and cream. Heat through and toss with cooked pasta. Top with chicken sauté and sprinkle with Parmesan cheese, if desired. Serve immediately.

*To make a bouquet garni, tie together 2 or 3 sprigs of parsley, 1 sprig of thyme and 2 or 3 bay leaves.*

# PORTOFINO
# PASTA

*Preparation time: 15 minutes*
*Cooking time: 20 minutes*
*4 servings*

| | | |
|---|---|---|
| 2 tbsp | vegetable oil | 30 mL |
| 4 | shallots or green onions, chopped | 4 |
| 1 cup | sliced zucchini | 250 mL |
| ½ lb | fresh or frozen shrimp, thawed | 250 g |
| ½ lb | boneless, skinless chicken breast, cut in strips | 250 g |
| 1 cup | broccoli florets | 250 mL |
| ¼ cup | dry white wine | 50 mL |
| ½ cup | cream (35% or 15%) | 125 mL |
| ½ tsp | *each* salt, pepper and dried thyme | 2 mL |
| 1 | tomato, peeled, seeded and chopped | 1 |
| 2 cups | rotini pasta | 500 mL |
| | grated Parmesan cheese | |

- Heat oil in large skillet over medium heat. Add shallots and zucchini. Cook 3 minutes, stirring occasionally. Add shrimp and cook 2 to 3 minutes, or until shrimp turn pink. With a slotted spoon, remove mixture from skillet and set aside.

- Place chicken in same skillet and cook 5 minutes, stirring occasionally. Add broccoli and continue cooking 3 to 4 minutes.

- Return shrimp mixture to skillet. Stir in white wine. Mix in cream, salt, pepper, thyme and tomato. Lower heat and simmer about 5 minutes, until sauce thickens slightly.

- Meanwhile, cook pasta in boiling salted water. Drain well and place in large serving bowl. Pour sauce over pasta and toss well. Serve with grated Parmesan cheese.

## TUSCANY CHICKEN

*Preparation time: 10 minutes*
*Cooking time: 50 minutes*
*6 servings*

| | | |
|---|---|---|
| 3 tbsp | olive oil | 45 mL |
| 6 | skinless chicken legs | 6 |
| 1 | medium onion, thinly sliced | 1 |
| 12 | garlic cloves, cut in quarters | 12 |
| 2 cups | canned stewed tomatoes | 500 mL |
| ½ cup | pitted black olives | 125 mL |
| ¼ cup | diced sun-dried tomatoes in oil | 50 mL |
| 1 tbsp | Italian seasoning | 15 mL |
| 1 tbsp | balsamic vinegar | 15 mL |
| | pinch hot pepper flakes (optional) | |
| | salt and pepper to taste | |

■ Heat oil over medium heat in large skillet or electric frying pan. Add chicken and brown on all sides. Remove from pan and set aside.

■ To same skillet, add onion and garlic; stir-fry until onion is soft. Add remaining ingredients and mix well. Add chicken. Cover pan and simmer over low heat 40 to 45 minutes or until chicken is no longer pink inside.

# LIGHTER MAIN MEALS

Chicken is not only a good source of nutrients, it's also low in calories, and that's important to today's cooks. In this chapter, we've included recipes that are especially low in fat, without being low in flavor!

Stir-fried, baked, barbecued or stewed, when it comes to chicken, the possibilities are endless. With just a few choice ingredients to bring out its full flavor, you can make healthy and delicious dinners in no time.

# CHICKEN WITH MUSHROOMS EN PAPILLOTE

*Preparation time: 15 minutes*
*Marinating time: 2 hours*
*Cooking time: 20 minutes*
*4 servings*

| | | |
|---|---|---|
| 4 | boneless, skinless chicken breast halves, cut in 3 pieces (1 lb/500 g) | 4 |
| 2 tbsp | soy sauce | 30 mL |
| 2 tsp | honey | 10 mL |
| 2 tbsp | sherry | 30 mL |
| ¼ tsp | five spice powder | 1 mL |
| 2 tsp | sesame oil | 10 mL |
| 1 tsp | grated fresh ginger | 5 mL |
| 4 | *each* shiitake and oyster mushrooms, diced | 4 |
| 1 | red bell pepper, cut in strips | 1 |
| ½ | zucchini, in julienne strips | 1 |
| 4 | green onions, chopped | 4 |
| | salt and pepper | |

- Place chicken in a bowl with soy sauce, honey, sherry, five spice powder, oil and ginger. Stir well. Cover and refrigerate 2 hours.

- Preheat oven to 350°F (180°C).

- Cut out four 10-inch (25 cm) circles of waxed parchment paper or aluminum foil.

- Drain chicken, discarding marinade. Arrange 3 pieces of chicken on each paper or foil circle. Top with mushrooms, bell pepper, zucchini and onions. Season with salt and pepper.

- Fold paper over chicken to make sealed envelopes. Arrange envelopes on baking sheet.

- Bake about 20 minutes, or until chicken is no longer pink inside.

# SESAME BAKED CHICKEN

*Preparation time: 5 minutes*
*Cooking time: 25 minutes*
*4 servings*

| | | |
|---|---|---|
| 8 | skinless chicken drumsticks | 8 |
| ¼ cup | honey | 50 mL |
| ¼ cup | sesame seeds | 50 mL |
| I tsp | finely chopped garlic | 5 mL |
| ¼ tsp | pepper | I mL |

- Preheat oven to 350°F (180°C). Arrange chicken in single layer in baking pan.

- Heat honey until warm. Brush over chicken.

- Combine sesame seeds, garlic and pepper. Sprinkle generously over chicken. Bake 25 to 30 minutes, basting occasionally with pan juices, until chicken is no longer pink inside.

## PEPPERY CLEMENTINE CHICKEN

**Preparation time: 5 minutes**
**Cooking time: 35 minutes**
**4 servings**

| | | |
|---|---|---|
| I tbsp | crushed peppercorns | 15 mL |
| 8 | skinless chicken thighs | 8 |
| I tbsp + I tsp | olive oil | 15 mL + 5 mL |
| I | shallot, finely chopped | I |
| I cup | clementine or orange juice | 250 mL |
| I tbsp | chopped orange zest | 15 mL |
| 2 tbsp | balsamic vinegar | 30 mL |
| I tsp | tomato paste | 5 mL |
| 2 | green onions, chopped | 2 |
| | salt | |
| | clementine or orange segments | |

■ Preheat oven to 350°F (180°C). Press peppercorns onto both sides of chicken.

■ Heat 1 tbsp (15 mL) oil in skillet over high heat. Cook chicken about 2 minutes each side until browned. Remove and arrange in baking pan. Bake 25 to 30 minutes.

■ Meanwhile, to same skillet over medium-high heat, add remaining oil. Add shallot and cook, stirring constantly, 1 minute.

■ Stir in juice, zest, vinegar and tomato paste. Bring to a boil, then lower heat to medium and cook until sauce is reduced by half.

■ When chicken is no longer pink inside, transfer to skillet along with cooking juices. Stir to coat with sauce. Add green onions and cook 2 to 3 minutes.

■ Season to taste with salt. Serve with clementine segments, wild rice and braised fennel, if desired.

# ALMOND CHICKEN
# WITH PRUNES

*Preparation time: 10 minutes*
*Cooking time: 40 minutes*
*4 to 6 servings*

| | | |
|---|---|---|
| 6 | skinless chicken legs | 6 |
| 1 tsp | salt | 5 mL |
| 1 tsp | pepper | 5 mL |
| 1 tsp | saffron or turmeric | 5 mL |
| 1 | cinnamon stick | 1 |
| 2 | onions, diced | 2 |
| 2 cups | chicken stock | 500 mL |
| 2 cups | pitted prunes | 500 mL |
| ¼ cup | honey | 50 mL |
| 1 tsp | cinnamon | 5 mL |
| ½ cup | toasted sliced almonds | 125 mL |

- Place chicken legs in a large saucepan with salt, pepper, saffron, cinnamon stick and onions. Add stock and bring to a boil over high heat. Lower heat and simmer 15 minutes, partially covered. Turn legs and continue cooking 15 minutes.

- When chicken is no longer pink inside, remove with slotted spoon and keep warm. Add prunes to pan and cook 5 to 10 minutes. Add honey and ground cinnamon. Cook until sauce thickens.

- Serve sauce over chicken, with couscous, if desired. Garnish with toasted almonds.

*Place chicken legs in a large saucepan with salt, pepper, saffron, cinnamon stick and onions.*

*Add stock and bring to a boil over high heat. Lower heat and simmer 15 minutes, partially covered.*

*Turn legs and continue cooking 15 minutes.*

*Remove chicken with slotted spoon and keep warm. Add prunes to pan and cook 5 to 10 minutes.*

*Add honey and ground cinnamon. Cook until sauce thickens.*

# CHICKEN, TOMATO AND
# BARLEY CASSEROLE

*Preparation time: 25 minutes*
*Cooking time: 45 minutes*
*6 servings*

| | | |
|---|---|---|
| 2 tbsp | corn oil | 30 mL |
| 1½ lbs | cubed chicken breast | 750 g |
| 2 | onions, halved and sliced | 2 |
| 2 cups | small mushrooms, quartered | 500 mL |
| 2 | red bell peppers, chopped | 2 |
| 1⅓ cups | pearl barley | 325 mL |
| I | can (28 oz/796 mL) crushed tomatoes | I |
| ¾ cup | chicken stock | 175 mL |
| 2 tsp | chopped fresh thyme | 10 mL |
| 2 tbsp | chopped fresh parsley | 30 mL |
| | salt and pepper | |

■ Preheat oven to 350°F (180°C).

■ In an oven-proof casserole, heat oil over high heat. Add chicken and brown 5 minutes.

■ Lower heat to medium. Add onions and cook 5 minutes. Add mushrooms and continue cooking 2 minutes, stirring constantly.

■ Add bell peppers, barley, tomatoes, stock and thyme. Season with salt and pepper; mix well.

■ Cover and bake in oven 30 minutes, or until barley is tender and liquid is absorbed. Sprinkle with parsley and serve.

# APRICOT GLAZED
# CHICKEN

*Preparation time: 10 minutes*
*Cooking time: 30 minutes*
*6 servings*

| | | |
|---|---|---|
| 2 tbsp | apricot jam | 30 mL |
| 1 tbsp | Dijon mustard | 15 mL |
| 1 tsp | chopped fresh tarragon | 5 mL |
| 6 | boneless, skinless chicken breast halves (1½ lbs/750 g) | 6 |

- Preheat oven to 350°F (180°C).

- In a small saucepan over low heat, combine jam, mustard and tarragon; stir just until jam melts.

- Arrange chicken in baking pan in single layer. (Pan should be just big enough to hold chicken.)

- Brush apricot sauce over chicken. Bake 30 minutes, or until chicken is tender, basting frequently with pan juices.

- Slice chicken and serve with potatoes and watercress, if desired.

# TANDOORI CHICKEN

*Preparation time: 10 minutes*
*Marinating time: 2 hours*
*Cooking time: 30 minutes*
*4 servings*

| | | |
|---|---|---:|
| 1 cup | plain yogurt | 250 mL |
| 2 | garlic cloves, finely chopped | 2 |
| 1 tsp | grated fresh ginger | 5 mL |
| 1 tsp | *each* curry powder and paprika | 5 mL |
| 1 tsp | *each* ground cumin and coriander | 5 mL |
| 4 | boneless, skinless chicken breast halves (1 lb/500 g) | 4 |
| 1 tbsp | vegetable oil | 15 mL |

- In a bowl, stir together yogurt, garlic, ginger and spices. Add chicken and stir to coat well. Let marinate 2 hours in refrigerator.
- Preheat oven to 350°F (180°C).
- Drain chicken pieces, discarding marinade. Heat oil in a skillet over medium-high heat. Add chicken and brown on all sides.
- Arrange chicken in baking pan. Bake 25 to 30 minutes.
- Serve with basmati rice and steamed vegetables, if desired.

## CHICKEN
## CHOP SUEY

*Preparation time: 20 minutes*
*Cooking time: 15 minutes*
*4 servings*

| | | |
|---|---|---|
| 1 tbsp | vegetable oil | 15 mL |
| 1 | onion, sliced | 1 |
| ½ | red bell pepper, cut in thin strips | ½ |
| ½ cup | celery sliced diagonally | 125 mL |
| 1 | carrot, peeled and sliced diagonally | 1 |
| 1 cup | snow peas | 250 mL |
| 1 lb | boneless, skinless chicken thighs, cut in strips | 500 g |
| 1 cup | quartered mushrooms | 250 mL |
| 1 | garlic clove, finely chopped | 1 |
| 2 lbs | bean sprouts | 1 kg |
| 2 tbsp | hoisin sauce | 30 mL |
| 1 tbsp | teriyaki sauce | 15 mL |
| 1 tbsp | finely chopped fresh ginger | 15 mL |
| | salt and pepper | |

- Heat oil in a large skillet or wok over high heat. Add onion, red pepper, celery, carrot and snowpeas. Stir-fry 3 to 4 minutes. Remove and keep warm.

- Add chicken to same skillet. Stir-fry 3 to 4 minutes. Add mushrooms, garlic and bean sprouts. Stir-fry 2 to 3 minutes.

- Combine remaining ingredients in a small bowl. Pour half of mixture over chicken and half over reserved vegetables. Let stand 2 to 3 minutes. Season with salt and pepper. Serve vegetables over chicken.

**Tip:** For a thicker sauce, dissolve 1 tbsp (15 mL) cornstarch into a little water and add to pan with hoisin sauce mixture.

LIGHTER MAIN MEALS

# CHICKEN AND VEGETABLE PACKAGES

**Preparation time: 15 minutes**
**Cooking time: 20 minutes**
**4 servings**

| | | |
|---|---|---|
| 4 | boneless, skinless chicken breast halves (1 lb/500 g) | 4 |
| 2 | lemons | 2 |
| 1 | potato, in julienne strips | 1 |
| 3 | carrots, in julienne strips | 3 |
| 1 | zucchini, in julienne strips | 1 |
| 2 tsp | fresh chopped thyme | 10 mL |
| | salt and pepper | |

- Preheat oven to 350°F (180°C).
- Cut four 10-inch (25 cm) squares of foil. Place one piece of chicken on each square.
- Cut 1 lemon into 8 thin slices. Arrange 2 slices on each piece of chicken.
- Arrange vegetables over chicken. Grate zest of remaining lemon over vegetables and spoon a little lemon juice over top. Sprinkle with thyme and season with salt and pepper.
- Fold foil over chicken and crimp edges to make a tight seal. Place packages on baking sheet. Bake 20 minutes, or until chicken is no longer pink inside.

Place 1 piece of chicken on each piece of foil. Top with 2 slices of lemon.

Arrange vegetables over chicken.

Grate zest of remaining lemon over vegetables and spoon lemon juice over top.

Fold foil over chicken.

Crimp edges of foil to make a tight seal.

# CHICKEN STEW
# WITH ROOT VEGETABLES

*Preparation time: 15 minutes*
*Cooking time: 45 minutes*
*4 to 6 servings*

| | | |
|---|---|---|
| 4 cups | chicken stock | 1 L |
| 1 | skinless whole chicken, cut in 8 | 1 |
| 2 | onions, quartered | 2 |
| ½ tsp | chopped fresh thyme | 2 mL |
| 2 | bay leaves | 2 |
| 2 | fresh sage sprigs | 2 |
| 12 | small new potatoes | 12 |
| 2 | medium turnips, peeled, halved and sliced | 2 |
| ½ | rutabaga, peeled and cubed | ½ |
| 6 | parsnips, peeled and sliced | 6 |
| 6 | baby carrots, peeled | 6 |
| | salt and pepper | |

- In a large stew pot, bring chicken stock to a boil. Add chicken, onion, thyme, bay leaves and sage. Season with salt and pepper. Cover and cook over medium heat 15 minutes.

- Add potatoes and turnips and continue cooking 10 minutes. Add rutabaga, parsnip and carrots and cook 15 minutes. When chicken is no longer pink inside, adjust seasonings and serve.

## CHICKEN WITH
## SORREL SAUCE

*Preparation time: 10 minutes*
*Cooking time: 25 minutes*
*4 servings*

| | | |
|---|---|---|
| 4 | skinless chicken breast halves (1 lb/500 g) | 4 |
| 2 tbsp | olive oil | 30 mL |
| 1 cup | fresh apple juice | 250 mL |
| 1 cup | chicken stock | 250 mL |
| 1 | bay leaf | 1 |
| 1 | bunch fresh sorrel, shredded | 1 |
| | salt and pepper | |

- Season chicken with salt and pepper. In skillet, brown chicken in olive oil over medium heat about 5 minutes.

- Add juice, stock and bay leaf. Cover and cook over low heat 10 minutes. Add sorrel and continue cooking 10 minutes until chicken is no longer pink inside.

- Adjust seasonings and serve immediately with steamed or grilled vegetables, if desired.

# MEDITERRANEAN
# CHICKEN

**Preparation time: 15 minutes**
**Cooking time: 35 minutes**
**4 servings**

| | | |
|---|---|---|
| 1 | onion | 1 |
| 1 | zucchini | 1 |
| ½ | small eggplant | ½ |
| 3 | Italian plum tomatoes | 3 |
| 2 tbsp | olive oil | 30 mL |
| 4 | boneless, skinless chicken breast halves (1 lb/500 g) | 4 |
| 1 tbsp | chopped fresh basil | 15 mL |
| ½ tsp | *each* chopped fresh oregano and marjoram | 2 mL |
| 1 to 2 | garlic cloves, finely chopped salt and pepper | 1 to 2 |

- Preheat oven to 350°F (180°C).

- Coarsely chop onion, zucchini, eggplant and tomatoes. Place 1 tbsp (15 mL) oil in large baking dish. Add vegetables and bake 7 to 8 minutes.

- Brush chicken with remaining olive oil and arrange on top of vegetables. Season with salt and pepper.

- Combine herbs and garlic. Sprinkle over chicken. Bake 25 to 30 minutes, until chicken is no longer pink inside. Serve with steamed potatoes, if desired.

**Note:** *This dish can also be prepared with chicken cutlets or boneless chicken thighs.*

# MIDDLE-EASTERN
# MARINATED CHICKEN

*Preparation time: 10 minutes*
*Marinating time: 2 hours*
*Cooking time: 20 minutes*
*4 servings*

| | | |
|---|---|---|
| ⅓ cup | red wine | 75 mL |
| 2 tbsp | olive oil | 30 mL |
| 2 tbsp | red wine vinegar | 30 mL |
| 1 | dash harissa sauce* | 1 |
| 1 | garlic clove, finely chopped | 1 |
| 1 tsp | *each* ground cumin and coriander | 5 mL |
| 8 | skinless chicken thighs | 8 |

■ In a small bowl, combine all ingredients except chicken. Set aside ¼-cup (50 mL) of wine mixture. Pour remaining mixture over chicken and marinate 2 hours.

■ Preheat barbecue to medium-high heat. Discard marinade and place chicken on barbecue rack 5 inches (12 cm) from heat. Cook 20 to 30 minutes, turning and basting early on with reserved wine mixture. Cook until chicken juices run clear.

*\* Harissa is a spicy condiment made from small peppers, cayenne, oil, garlic, cilantro, cumin and mint or verbena leaves.*

# TROPICAL CHICKEN
# BROCHETTES

*Preparation time: 20 minutes*
*Marinating time: 1 hour*
*Cooking time: 10 minutes*
*4 servings*

| | | |
|---|---|---|
| ⅓ cup | fresh lime juice | 75 mL |
| 1 tsp | grated lime zest | 5 mL |
| 2 tbsp | vegetable oil | 30 mL |
| 2 tbsp | honey | 30 mL |
| 2 tbsp | unsweetened grated coconut | 30 mL |
| 1 tbsp | finely chopped fresh ginger | 15 mL |
| 1 | garlic clove, finely chopped | 1 |
| 1 lb | cubed chicken breast | 500 g |
| 1 | red bell pepper, cut in 1-inch (2.5 cm) pieces | 1 |
| ½ | fresh pineapple, cut in 1-inch (2.5 cm) pieces | ½ |

■ In a large airtight plastic container, stir together lime juice and zest, oil, honey, coconut, ginger and garlic. Reserve ¼-cup (50 mL) for basting. Add chicken to remaining lime mixture, stir well to coat, and cover tightly. Refrigerate 1 hour.

■ Discard marinade and thread chicken onto skewers, alternating with pieces of red pepper and pineapple. Preheat barbecue to medium-high heat.

■ Place brochettes on oiled grill about 5 inches (12 cm) from heat. Cook 10 to 12 minutes or until chicken juices run clear. Baste early on with reserved lime mixture and turn brochettes halfway through cooking time. Serve with rice, if desired.

**Note:** *Brochettes can also be grilled under broiler in oven.*

# SPECIAL OCCASIONS

Preparing an elegant dinner for family or friends does not have to be difficult and time-consuming, especially when chicken plays the starring role. This chapter presents a whole host of simple yet refined recipes to charm and impress your guests.

Featuring new cuts of chicken and special ingredients like balsamic vinegar or sun-dried tomatoes, these mouth-watering dishes are sure to please everyone. In fact, why wait for a special occasion?

# RASPBERRY CHICKEN
## TOURNEDOS

*Preparation time: 30 minutes*
*Marinating time: 2 hours*
*Cooking time: 30 minutes*
*4 servings*

| | | |
|---|---|---|
| ½ cup | vegetable oil | 125 mL |
| ¼ cup | raspberry vinegar | 50 mL |
| 1 tbsp | chopped fresh thyme | 15 mL |
| 4 | tournedos-style chicken breast halves* (1 lb/500 g) | 4 |
| 1 tbsp | vegetable oil | 15 mL |
| 2 tbsp | raspberry vinegar | 30 mL |
| 1 cup | chicken stock | 250 mL |
| 1 tbsp | Meaux or Dijon mustard | 15 mL |
| ¾ cup | heavy cream (35%) | 175 mL |
| ½ cup | fresh raspberries | 125 mL |
| | salt and pepper | |

- Mix together oil, ¼-cup (50 mL) vinegar and thyme; season with salt and pepper. Pour mixture over chicken, cover and marinate in refrigerator 2 to 4 hours, turning chicken every hour.

- Preheat oven to 350°F (180°C).

- Remove chicken from marinade and pat dry with paper towels. In a skillet, heat 1 tbsp (15 mL) oil over high heat. Add chicken and brown on both sides.

- Transfer to a baking dish. Bake 20 minutes, or until juices run clear. Remove tournedos and keep warm.

- Discard fat in baking dish. Add remaining 2 tbsp (30 mL) vinegar; cook on stove top over medium heat, stirring constantly, until reduced by half. Add chicken stock and mustard. Continue cooking until reduced by half again.

- Stir in cream; season with salt and pepper. Divide sauce between 4 plates and place chicken tournedos on top. Garnish with raspberries and serve with pattypan squash and wild mushrooms, if desired.

*Tournedos-style chicken breast halves are wrapped in bacon and tied with kitchen string. You can also use boneless, skinless chicken breast halves.*

# BALSAMIC CHICKEN
# WITH PEARS

*Preparation time: 10 minutes*
*Cooking time: 20 minutes*
*4 servings*

| | | |
|---|---|---|
| 1 tbsp | vegetable oil | 15 mL |
| 4 | boneless, skinless chicken breast halves (1 lb/500g) | 4 |
| 1 tbsp | butter | 15 mL |
| 3 | fresh pears, peeled, cored and cut in 8 | 3 |
| 3 tbsp | balsamic vinegar | 45 mL |
| ½ cup | chicken stock | 125 mL |
| | salt and pepper | |

■ Preheat oven to 350°F (180°C). Heat oil in a skillet over medium-high heat. Add chicken. Season with salt and pepper. Cook about 6 minutes each side, or until no longer pink inside. Remove from skillet and keep warm in oven.

■ Wipe skillet clean then add butter. Add pears and cook over high heat about 4 minutes, until lightly browned. Add vinegar and chicken stock. Bring to a boil, lower heat and let simmer 1 minute.

■ Return chicken to skillet. Cook over high heat 1 minute, stirring constantly, until sauce thickens slightly. Slice and serve with asparagus, if desired.

# GLAZED CHICKEN WITH
# CRANBERRY SAUCE

*Preparation time: 10 minutes*
*Cooking time: 30 minutes*
*4 servings*

| | | |
|---|---|---|
| 1 tsp | sesame oil | 5 mL |
| 1 cup | cranberry jelly | 250 mL |
| 2 tbsp | soy sauce | 30 mL |
| 1 tbsp | fresh lemon juice | 15 mL |
| 2 tsp | grated fresh ginger | 10 mL |
| 4 | boneless, skinless chicken breast halves (1 lb/500 g) | 4 |
| | salt and pepper to taste | |

## Cranberry Orange Sauce:

| | | |
|---|---|---|
| 2 cups | fresh cranberries | 500 mL |
| 1 cup | orange juice | 250 mL |
| ⅓ cup | sugar | 75 mL |
| 1½ tsp | balsamic or cider vinegar | 7 mL |
| 1 tsp | grated orange zest | 5 mL |
| 1 | envelope (about 1 oz/30 g) gravy mix | 1 |

- Preheat oven to 400°F (200°C). In a large bowl or blender, combine oil, cranberry jelly, soy sauce, lemon juice, ginger, salt and pepper; blend until smooth.

- Brush mixture over chicken. Bake 30 minutes, or until juices run clear, basting with mixture every 10 minutes.

- Meanwhile, in a saucepan, stir together all cranberry orange sauce ingredients except gravy. Bring to a boil, then lower heat and cook 5 to 7 minutes, stirring occasionally, until cranberries burst.

- Mix gravy according to package instructions. Add to cranberry orange sauce and cook 5 minutes to thicken. Keep warm.

- Serve glazed chicken with cranberry orange sauce, green beans, fennel and wild rice, if desired.

# COQ AU VIN

***Preparation time: 10 minutes***
***Cooking time: 1 hour***
***4 servings***

| | | |
|---|---|---|
| 3 tbsp | all-purpose flour | 45 mL |
| ½ tsp | paprika | 2 mL |
| ½ tsp | salt | 2 mL |
| 4 | skinless chicken legs | 4 |
| 2 tbsp | oil | 30 mL |
| ¼ cup | brandy | 50 mL |
| 12 | pearl onions | 12 |
| ½ lb | mushrooms, halved | 250 g |
| 1 | garlic clove, finely chopped | 1 |
| 2 tbsp | chopped fresh parsley | 30 mL |
| 1 | bay leaf | 1 |
| ½ tsp | dried marjoram | 2 mL |
| ½ tsp | dried thyme | 2 mL |
| 1 cup | dry red wine | 250 mL |
| | pinch of mace | |

- Mix flour, paprika, mace and salt in a plastic bag. Add chicken legs and shake to coat chicken.

- Heat oil in a large skillet over medium heat. Add chicken and brown on both sides. Turn off heat. Add brandy and ignite. Once flames die out, remove chicken and set aside.

- Increase heat under same skillet to medium-high. Add onions, mushrooms and garlic; sauté 2 to 3 minutes. Stir in parsley, bay leaf, marjoram, thyme and wine.

- Reduce heat to low. Return chicken legs to skillet; cover and simmer 45 minutes to 1 hour, or until chicken is tender. Serve with carrots and potatoes, if desired.

*Mix flour, paprika, mace and salt in a plastic bag. Add chicken legs and shake to coat chicken.*

*Heat oil in a large skillet over medium heat. Add chicken and brown on both sides.*

*Increase heat under same skillet to medium-high. Add onions, mushrooms and garlic; sauté 2 to 3 minutes.*

*Stir in parsley, bay leaf, marjoram, thyme and wine.*

*Return chicken legs to skillet; cover and simmer until chicken is tender, 45 minutes to 1 hour.*

## ROAST CHICKEN
## WITH PORT

*Preparation time: 10 minutes*
*Cooking time: 50 minutes*
*4 servings*

| | | |
|---|---|---|
| 1 tbsp | vegetable oil | 15 mL |
| 4 | tournedos-style chicken thighs* (1 lb/500 g) | 4 |
| ½ cup | port wine | 125 mL |
| 1 | shallot, finely chopped | 1 |
| 1 cup | quartered mushrooms | 250 mL |
| ½ cup | table cream (15%) | 125 mL |
| | salt and pepper | |

■ Preheat oven to 350°F (180°C). In a saucepan, heat oil over high heat. Add chicken thighs and brown on all sides about 5 minutes. Season with salt and pepper. Transfer to roasting pan and cook in oven 20 to 25 minutes, or until juices run clear.

■ When thighs are done, remove from pan and keep warm in oven. Add port to juices in roasting pan and cook on stove over high heat 3 minutes.

■ Add shallot and mushrooms; continue cooking until reduced by half. Add cream and season with salt and pepper. Continue cooking 1 minute.

■ Slice thighs and top with sauce. Serve with greens and sweet potatoes, if desired.

*\* Tournedos-style chicken thighs are wrapped in bacon and tied with kitchen string. You can also use boneless, skinless chicken thighs or chicken breast halves.*

# CHICKEN WITH WHITE WINE
# AND APPLES

*Preparation time: 20 minutes*
*Cooking time: 35 minutes*
*4 servings*

| | | |
|---|---|---|
| 4 | boneless, skinless chicken breast halves (1 lb/500 g) | 4 |
| ¼ cup | all-purpose flour | 50 mL |
| 1 tbsp | butter | 15 mL |
| 1 tbsp | oil | 15 mL |
| ½ cup | white wine or dry cider | 125 mL |
| 2 cups | pearl onions | 500 mL |
| 1 lb | small mushrooms, halved | 500 g |
| 2 | celery stalks, sliced | 2 |
| 2 | red apples, peeled, cored and diced | 2 |
| 1¼ cups | chicken stock | 300 mL |
| ½ cup | 15% or 35% cream | 125 mL |
| | flour | |
| | salt and pepper | |

- Coat chicken with flour. Heat butter and oil in a large skillet. Brown chicken on both sides over medium-high heat, about 5 minutes. Remove chicken and keep warm. Pour out fat from skillet.

- Add wine to skillet. Simmer until reduced by half.

- Return chicken to skillet. Add onions, mushrooms, celery, apples and chicken stock; season with salt and pepper. Cover and simmer gently about 15 minutes.

- With slotted spoon, remove chicken and vegetables; keep warm. Add cream to pan juices and simmer about 10 minutes to thicken. Serve sauce over chicken and vegetables.

# HAZELNUT CHICKEN
# WITH CARAMELIZED ONIONS

*Preparation time: 15 minutes*
*Cooking time: 15 minutes*
*6 servings*

| | | |
|---|---|---|
| 6 | boneless, skinless chicken breast halves (1½ lbs/750 g) | 6 |
| ½ cup | all-purpose flour | 125 mL |
| 2 | eggs | 2 |
| ½ tsp | salt | 2 mL |
| ½ tsp | pepper | 2 mL |
| 2 cups | fresh breadcrumbs | 500 mL |
| 1½ cups | toasted hazelnuts or almonds, finely chopped | 375 mL |
| 1 tbsp | butter | 15 mL |
| 1 tbsp | oil | 15 mL |

**Onion Sauce:**

| | | |
|---|---|---|
| 2 tbsp | butter | 30 mL |
| 3 | large onions, halved and sliced | 3 |
| 1 cup | chicken stock | 250 mL |
| 2 tsp | chopped fresh rosemary | 10 mL |

- Coat chicken on all sides with flour.

- Beat together eggs, salt and pepper. In another bowl, stir together breadcrumbs and nuts. Dip chicken in egg, then in crumbs to coat well.

- Preheat oven to 375°F (190°C). Heat butter and oil in a skillet over medium heat. Add chicken and cook until golden brown on both sides. Transfer to baking sheet and bake 20 minutes, or until juices run clear.

- Meanwhile, to make the sauce, melt 2 tbsp (30 mL) butter over medium heat. Add onions and cook 20 minutes, stirring occasionally. When onions begin to caramelize, add chicken stock and rosemary. Bring to a boil, lower heat and simmer until ready to serve.

- Slice chicken and serve with onion sauce, Swiss chard and wild mushrooms, if desired.

# FRENCH COUNTRY CHICKEN

*Preparation time: 10 minutes*
*Cooking time: 1 hour*
*4 servings*

| | | |
|---|---|---|
| 1 | 2-lb (1 kg) chicken, cut in 8 pieces | 1 |
| 1 tsp | salt | 5 mL |
| ½ tsp | paprika | 2 mL |
| ¼ tsp | pepper | 1 mL |
| 1 tbsp | butter | 15 mL |
| 1 tbsp | oil | 15 mL |
| 2 cups | sliced mushrooms | 500 mL |
| 1 | small onion, chopped | 1 |
| 2 tbsp | all-purpose flour | 30 mL |
| ¾ cup | dry white wine | 175 mL |
| ¾ cup | chicken stock | 175 mL |
| 1 tbsp | chopped fresh thyme | 15 mL |
| 1 | jar (12 oz/340 mL) artichoke bottoms, drained and quartered | 1 |

- Combine salt, paprika and pepper; sprinkle over chicken pieces.
- Heat butter and oil in a skillet. Cook chicken 5 minutes each side over medium-high heat. Transfer chicken to baking dish.
- Preheat oven to 350°F (180°C).
- To same skillet, add mushrooms and onion. Cook 5 minutes.
- Sprinkle in flour and stir well. Gradually add wine, chicken stock and thyme. Bring to a boil, then simmer 5 minutes until thickened. Pour over chicken.
- Bake chicken uncovered, about 30 minutes. Add artichoke bottoms and continue baking 15 minutes, or until chicken is tender. Serve with steamed vegetables.

*Heat butter and oil in a skillet. Cook chicken over medium-high heat until browned. Transfer to baking dish.*

*To same skillet, add mushrooms and onion. Cook 5 minutes.*

*Sprinkle in flour and stir well.*

Gradually add wine, stock and thyme. Bring to a boil then simmer 5 minutes until thickened.

Pour mushroom sauce over chicken and bake about 30 minutes.

Add artichoke bottoms and continue baking 15 minutes, or until chicken is tender.

145

## CHICKEN WITH CHÈVRE AND APPLESAUCE

**Preparation time: 20 minutes**
**Cooking time: 25 minutes**
**4 servings**

| | | |
|---|---|---|
| 1 tbsp | butter | 15 mL |
| 4 | boneless, skinless chicken breast halves (1 lb/500 g) or 8 chicken thighs | 4 |
| ½ cup | unsweetened apple juice | 125 mL |
| 1 cup | chicken stock | 250 mL |
| 2 | fresh apples, peeled, cored and thinly sliced | 2 |
| 1 | log (8 oz/160 g) soft goats' cheese (chèvre) | 1 |
| | salt and pepper | |
| | chopped fresh parsley | |

- In a saucepan, heat butter over medium-high heat. Add chicken and cook on both sides until golden, about 5 minutes. Add apple juice, chicken stock and apple slices. Season with salt and pepper.

- Bring to a boil, then cover and simmer over low heat about 5 minutes. Turn chicken and continue cooking 10 minutes, or until juices run clear. Remove chicken and set aside; keep apple sauce warm.

- Preheat oven to 350°F (180°C). Cut goats' cheese into rounds and coat with parsley.

- Slice chicken and alternate chicken and cheese slices on 6 oven-proof plates. Place in oven a few minutes to warm the cheese.

- Pour sauce with apples around each serving. Garnish with tarragon sprigs, if desired.

# SAGE CHICKEN TOURNEDOS
# WITH FRESH FIGS

*Preparation time: 15 minutes*
*Cooking time: 25 minutes*
*4 servings*

| | | |
|---|---|---|
| 1 tbsp | vegetable oil | 15 mL |
| 4 | tournedos-style chicken breast halves* (1 lb/500 g) | 4 |
| 2 | shallots, finely chopped | 2 |
| 2 | fresh figs, cut in 6 | 2 |
| 2 tbsp | maple syrup | 30 mL |
| 1 cup | chicken stock | 250 mL |
| 1 tsp | chopped fresh sage | 5 mL |
| | salt and pepper | |

- Preheat oven to 350°F (180°C). In a saucepan, heat oil over medium-high heat. Add chicken and cook 2 to 3 minutes each side. Season with salt and pepper.
- Transfer chicken to baking dish and bake about 20 minutes, or until no longer pink inside.
- Meanwhile, in the same saucepan, cook shallots, figs and maple syrup over medium heat until slightly caramelized, about 5 minutes. Add chicken stock and continue cooking until reduced by half. Lower heat, add sage and simmer a few minutes.
- Pour sauce over chicken tournedos and serve with zucchini, if desired.

*Tournedos-style chicken breast halves are wrapped in bacon and tied with kitchen string. You can also use boneless, skinless chicken breast halves.*

## CREAMY DIJON
## CHICKEN

**Preparation time: 10 minutes**
**Cooking time: 10 minutes**
**4 servings**

| | | |
|---|---|---|
| 4 | boneless, skinless chicken breast halves (1 lb/500 g) | 4 |
| ¼ cup | all-purpose flour | 50 mL |
| 1 tbsp | vegetable oil | 15 mL |
| 1 tbsp | butter | 15 mL |
| ½ cup | chicken stock | 125 mL |
| ¼ cup | dry sherry or dry white wine | 50 mL |
| ¼ cup | table cream (15%) | 50 mL |
| 2 tbsp | Dijon mustard | 30 mL |
| | salt and pepper | |

■ Place chicken breast halves between 2 sheets of waxed paper. Pound with a wooden mallet or flat side of a large knife until ½-inch (1 cm) thick.

■ Coat chicken on both sides with flour. Heat oil and butter together in large skillet over medium heat. Brown chicken 5 minutes on each side. Remove and keep warm.

■ Drain grease from skillet. Stir in stock and sherry. Cook over low heat until reduced slightly. Stir in cream and mustard. Simmer over low heat 2 to 3 minutes or until thickened.

■ Season with salt and pepper. Pour sauce over chicken and serve with new potatoes and greens.

# CHICKEN AND PORK ROAST WITH LEEKS

**Preparation time: 15 minutes**
**Cooking time: 50 minutes**
**4 servings**

| | | |
|---|---|---|
| 1 | chicken breast roast stuffed with pork tenderloin* (1 lb/500 g) | 1 |
| 1 tbsp | Dijon mustard | 15 mL |
| 1 tbsp | vegetable oil | 15 mL |
| 2 tsp | olive oil | 10 mL |
| 2 | leeks, white part only, in julienne strips | 2 |
| 1 tbsp | all-purpose flour | 15 mL |
| ½ cup | dry white wine or apple juice | 125 mL |
| 1 cup | chicken stock | 250 mL |
| ½ cup | table cream (15%) salt and pepper | 125 mL |

- Preheat oven to 350°F (180°C). Brush chicken with mustard; season with salt and pepper. Heat vegetable oil in large saucepan over medium-high heat. Add chicken and brown on all sides, about 5 minutes.
- Transfer to roasting pan and cook in oven 45 to 50 minutes or until juices run clear.
- When chicken is almost done, heat olive oil in a saucepan over medium heat. Add leek and sauté 5 minutes. Add flour, wine and chicken stock; let simmer until sauce thickens. Season with salt and pepper. Remove from heat and stir in cream.
- Slice roast and serve over sauce.

*Chicken 'roasts' are boneless chicken breasts or thighs that can be stuffed with pork or veal. If you can't find them, ask your butcher to prepare them for you. You can also use boneless, skinless chicken breast halves or roasts that are not stuffed. Simply reduce the cooking time by 5 minutes.

# CITRUS CHICKEN WITH
# MUSHROOMS AND GRUYÈRE

*Preparation time: 20 minutes*
*Marinating time: 30 minutes*
*Cooking time: 40 minutes*

| | | |
|---|---|---|
| 4 | boneless, skinless chicken breast halves (1 lb/500 g) | 4 |
| 1 | lemon | 1 |
| 1 | orange | 1 |
| 1 | grapefruit | 1 |
| 1 | lime | 1 |
| ⅓ cup | vegetable oil | 75 mL |
| 2 tbsp | Dijon mustard | 30 mL |
| 1 tbsp | butter | 15 mL |
| 1 | shallot, chopped | 1 |
| ½ lb | mushrooms, finely chopped | 250 g |
| 1 cup | grated Gruyère, Swiss or Emmenthal cheese | 250 mL |
| 1 tbsp | chopped fresh tarragon salt and pepper | 15 mL |

- Flatten chicken pieces with wooden mallet and arrange in shallow baking dish. Peel fruit and chop zest. Squeeze juice from fruit into small bowl. Add oil, mustard and chopped zest. Pour over chicken and marinate 30 minutes in refrigerator.

- Meanwhile, melt butter in saucepan over medium heat. Add shallot and mushrooms; cook 10 minutes, stirring constantly. Let cool and transfer to small bowl. Add grated cheese and tarragon; mix well.

- Preheat oven to 350°F (180°C). Drain chicken pieces, discarding marinade, and pat dry with paper towels.

- Distribute cheese mixture over chicken pieces; season with salt and pepper. Roll to enclose filling and hold in place with kitchen string or toothpicks.

- Bake about 30 minutes, or until juice from chicken runs clear. Slice and serve over pasta, if desired.

*Peel citrus fruit and chop zest.*

*Squeeze juice from fruit into small bowl. Add oil, mustard and chopped zest.*

*Cook shallot and mushrooms in melted butter 10 minutes, stirring constantly.*

Add grated cheese and
tarragon; mix well.

Distribute cheese mixture
over chicken pieces; season
with salt and pepper.

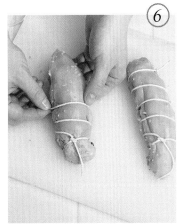

Roll chicken to enclose
filling and hold in place
with kitchen string.

# CHICKEN AND VEGETABLE ROLLS
# WITH FRESH HERBS

*Preparation time: 20 minutes*
*Chilling time: 20 minutes*
*Cooking time: 30 minutes*
*6 servings*

## Stuffing:

| | | |
|---|---|---|
| ½ lb | ground chicken | 250 g |
| 2 tbsp | heavy cream (35%) | 30 mL |
| I | shallot, finely chopped | I |
| I tsp | chopped fresh parsley | 5 mL |
| | salt and pepper to taste | |

## Rolls:

| | | |
|---|---|---|
| I | carrot, in julienne strips | I |
| I | zucchini, in julienne strips | I |
| I2 | green beans | I2 |
| 6 | boneless, skinless chicken breast halves (1½ lbs/750 g) | 6 |
| I tbsp | butter or oil | I5 mL |
| ½ cup | white wine | I25 mL |
| I cup | heavy cream (35%) | 250 mL |
| I tbsp | *each* chopped fresh parsley, tarragon and basil | I5 mL |
| I | garlic clove, finely chopped | I |
| | salt and pepper | |

- Combine all stuffing ingredients. Refrigerate 20 minutes.
- Preheat oven to 350°F (180°C). Cook vegetables in boiling water 1 minute. Drain and rinse under cold water.
- Flatten chicken pieces with wooden mallet. Divide stuffing evenly over chicken. Top with vegetables. Roll chicken to enclose vegetables and tie with kitchen string.
- Heat butter in skillet over medium-high heat. Brown chicken rolls on all sides.
- Transfer rolls to baking dish and bake 20 to 25 minutes, until tender. Remove from oven and cut strings. Keep warm.
- Meanwhile, to same skillet add wine and cook until reduced by half. Stir in cream, fresh herbs and garlic. Season with salt and pepper; cook 2 to 3 minutes.
- Cut chicken rolls in half and serve with cream sauce, braised endives and Brussels sprouts, if desired.

# CHICKEN STUFFED WITH CHEESE AND SUN-DRIED TOMATOES

*Preparation time: 15 minutes*
*Cooking time: 20 minutes*
*4 servings*

| | | |
|---|---|---|
| ½ cup | Ricotta cheese | 125 mL |
| ¼ cup | soft goats' cheese | 50 mL |
| 1 tbsp | butter | 15 mL |
| 10 oz | fresh spinach, finely chopped | 300 g |
| 1 | garlic clove, finely chopped | 1 |
| 4 | boneless, skinless chicken breast halves (1 lb/500 g) | 4 |
| 16 | sun-dried tomatoes in oil | 16 |
| ¼ cup | 35% or 15% cream | 50 mL |
| 1 cup | chicken stock | 250 mL |
| ¼ tsp | ground nutmeg | 1 mL |
| | salt and pepper | |

- In a bowl, stir together Ricotta and goats' cheese.

- Heat butter in a saucepan. Add spinach and garlic. Cover and cook over high heat, about 2 minutes. Let cool.

- Stir half of spinach into cheese mixture. Season with salt and pepper. Set aside remaining spinach for sauce.

- Slice chicken open across the thickness and flatten with a mallet. Spread ¼ of cheese mixture on one side of each chicken piece. Top each piece with 4 sun-dried tomatoes. Fold closed and hold in place with toothpicks or kitchen string.

- Broil chicken in oven 5 inches (12 cm) from heat, about 8 minutes on each side.

- Meanwhile, in saucepan, combine cream, chicken stock, nutmeg and reserved spinach. Bring to a boil then let simmer 3 to 4 minutes. Process until smooth in blender or food processor. Season with salt and pepper.

- Slice chicken and serve over cream sauce, with fresh pasta, if desired.

# APRICOT CHICKEN
# AND PORK ROAST

**Preparation time: 15 minutes**
**Cooking time: 45 minutes**
**4 servings**

| | | |
|---|---|---|
| 1 tbsp | peanut oil | 15 mL |
| 4 | chicken breast roasts stuffed with pork tenderloin* (7 oz/210 g *each*) | 4 |
| 1 tbsp | butter | 15 mL |
| 1 tbsp | vegetable oil | 15 mL |
| 1 | red onion, very thinly sliced | 1 |
| 12 | dried apricots, halved | 12 |
| 1 cup | white wine | 250 mL |
| ¼ cup | Calvados or brandy | 50 mL |
| 1 | bouquet garni** | 1 |
| | salt and pepper | |

* *Chicken 'roasts' are boneless chicken breasts or thighs that can be stuffed with pork or veal. If you can't find them, ask your butcher to prepare them for you. You can also use boneless, skinless chicken breast halves or roasts that aren't stuffed. Simply reduce the cooking time by 5 minutes.*

■ Preheat oven to 350°F (180°C). In a large saucepan, heat peanut oil over medium-high heat. Add roasts and cook until browned on all sides, about 5 minutes. Season with salt and pepper; transfer to a roasting pan.

■ In same skillet, heat butter and vegetable oil. Add onion and cook over low heat 2 to 3 minutes. Add apricots and continue cooking 1 minute.

■ Add white wine and Calvados; bring to a boil. Pour over roasts and add bouquet garni. Cook in oven 35 to 40 minutes.

■ Remove roasts from oven, cut strings and slice. Season with salt and pepper. Serve with mashed potatoes and steamed broccoli, if desired.

** *To make a simple bouquet garni, tie together 2 or 3 sprigs of parsley, 1 sprig of thyme and 2 or 3 bay leaves.*

# WHOLE ROASTED CHICKEN WITH RICE AND PINE NUT STUFFING

*Preparation time: 25 minutes*
*Cooking time: 1 hour and 50 minutes*
*4 to 6 servings*

| | | |
|---|---|---|
| 1 tbsp | vegetable oil | 15 mL |
| ¼ lb | chicken livers, washed, trimmed and diced | 125 g |
| 3 tbsp | pine nuts | 45 mL |
| 1 tbsp | butter | 15 mL |
| 1 | medium onion, chopped | 1 |
| 1 | leek, white part only, chopped | 1 |
| 1 cup | long grain rice | 250 mL |
| 4 cups | chicken stock | 1 L |
| ¼ cup | currants | 50 mL |
| ¼ cup | dried cranberries | 50 mL |
| 1 tbsp | chopped fresh thyme | 15 mL |
| 2 tbsp | butter | 30 mL |
| 1 | whole chicken (3 lbs/1.5 kg) salt and pepper | 1 |

■ In a saucepan, heat oil over high heat. Add livers and pine nuts; cook, stirring constantly, about 5 minutes until pine nuts are golden; set aside.

■ Heat 1 tbsp (15 mL) butter in another saucepan over medium heat. Add onion and leek and cook about 5 minutes. Add livers, nuts and rice; Cook, stirring constantly, to coat rice.

■ Add chicken stock, currants, cranberries and thyme; season with salt and pepper. Bring to a boil then let simmer 20 to 25 minutes over medium heat, or until rice has absorbed all liquid. Add 2 tbsp (30 mL) butter and toss.

■ Preheat oven to 400°F (200°C). Pat chicken dry with paper towels and stuff with rice mixture. Close chicken with toothpicks or tie with kitchen string. Season with salt and pepper. Transfer to roasting pan and cook in oven 15 minutes.

■ Lower oven temperature to 350°F (180°C). Continue cooking chicken 1 hour, or until chicken juices run clear.

# SIMPLE SAUCES AND STOCKS

With so many different ways to prepare it and so many complementary flavors, chicken is truly one of the most versatile foods. Sautéed in sauce or simply barbecued, chicken stays light and full of flavor.

This chapter presents a dozen simple ways to enhance the flavor of chicken with sauces and marinades. It also includes two recipes for chicken stock, which provides the basis for all kinds of savory soups and is always better when prepared from scratch.

## SPICY TOMATO
## BARBECUE SAUCE

*Preparation time: 10 minutes*
*Cooking time: 30 minutes*
*Makes 3 cups (750 mL)*

| | | |
|---|---|---|
| 1 | can tomatoes with juice (28 oz/796 mL) | 1 |
| 1½ cups | chopped onion | 375 mL |
| 1 cup | diced red bell pepper | 250 mL |
| 1 | large garlic clove, crushed | 1 |
| ½ cup | cider vinegar | 125 mL |
| ½ cup | packed brown sugar | 125 mL |
| 1 tbsp | chili powder | 15 mL |
| 2 tsp | mustard powder | 10 mL |
| 1 tsp | Tabasco sauce | 5 mL |
| ¼ tsp | *each* ground ginger, cinnamon and cloves | 1 mL |
| ⅓ cup | vegetable oil | 75 mL |

- Pour tomatoes into large, heavy saucepan and crush with a potato masher. Add all remaining ingredients except oil.

- Bring mixture to a boil. Reduce heat to medium and let simmer 30 to 35 minutes, stirring frequently, until thickened.

- Pour mixture into food processor or blender; blend until smooth.

- Return to saucepan and stir in vegetable oil; bring to a boil.

- Use immediately or pour into sterilized, airtight jars. Sauce will keep several weeks in the refrigerator.

# TRADITIONAL
# BARBECUE SAUCE

*Preparation time: 10 minutes*
*Makes 1¼ cups (300 mL)*

| | | |
|---|---|---|
| ½ cup | ketchup | 125 mL |
| ½ cup | chili sauce | 125 mL |
| 1 tbsp | Dijon mustard | 15 mL |
| 1 tbsp | brown sugar | 15 mL |
| 1 tbsp | vinegar | 15 mL |
| 1 tbsp | soy sauce | 15 mL |
| 1 tbsp | Worcestershire sauce | 15 mL |
| 1 | garlic clove, finely chopped | 1 |
| 1 tsp | Tabasco sauce | 5 mL |

- Combine all ingredients and mix well. Baste chicken pieces during last 15 minutes of barbecuing.

# SENSATIONAL
# BARBECUE SAUCE WITH BEER

*Preparation time: 15 minutes*
*Cooking time: 5 minutes*
*Makes 3 cups (750 mL)*

| | | |
|---|---|---|
| 2 tbsp | vegetable oil | 30 mL |
| 1 | large onion, chopped | 1 |
| 2 | garlic cloves, crushed | 2 |
| 1 | can tomato paste (5½ oz/156 mL) | 1 |
| ¾ cup | beer | 175 mL |
| ¼ cup | brown sugar | 50 mL |
| 1 tbsp | Worcestershire sauce | 15 mL |
| 2 tsp | prepared horseradish | 10 ml |
| 2 tsp | Dijon mustard | 10 mL |
| 1 tsp | dried tarragon | 5 mL |
| 1 tsp | dried thyme | 5 mL |
| 2 to 3 | drops hot pepper sauce | 2 to 3 |

- Heat oil in a saucepan over medium heat. Add onion and cook until soft, about 10 minutes. Add garlic; cook 2 minutes.
- Stir in remaining ingredients and let simmer 5 minutes.
- Baste chicken pieces during last 15 minutes of barbecuing.

# MARVELOUS
# MARINADES

## To prepare a marinade:

- Stir together all ingredients. Set aside ¼-cup (50 mL) of mixture for basting. Marinate chicken pieces in remaining mixture 2 hours in the refrigerator.
- Discard marinade. Cook marinated chicken pieces over medium-high heat on the barbecue or under the broiler.
- Baste frequently early in the cooking process with reserved mixture. Cook until chicken juices run clear when pierced with a fork.

## SWEET AND SOUR MARINADE

| | | |
|---|---|---|
| ½ cup | teriyaki sauce | 125 mL |
| ½ cup | peanut oil | 125 mL |
| ¼ cup | soy sauce | 50 mL |
| ¼ cup | white wine vinegar | 50 mL |
| 2 | garlic cloves, finely chopped | 2 |
| 2 | green onions, chopped | 2 |
| 2 tbsp | ketchup | 30 mL |
| 2 tsp | maple syrup | 10 mL |
| | salt and pepper | |

## ORANGE SESAME MARINADE

| | | |
|---|---|---|
| 3 tbsp | frozen concentrated orange juice, thawed | 45 mL |
| 2 tbsp | soy sauce | 30 mL |
| 2 tbsp | honey | 30 mL |
| 2 tbsp | marmalade | 30 mL |
| 1 tbsp | sesame oil | 15 mL |
| 1 | garlic clove, finely chopped | 1 |
| 1 tbsp | finely chopped fresh ginger | 15 mL |
| 2 tbsp | sesame seeds | 30 mL |

## LEMON MUSTARD MARINADE

| | | |
|---|---|---|
| 3 tbsp | Dijon mustard | 45 mL |
| 2 | green onions, finely chopped | 2 |
| 2 tbsp | fresh lemon juice | 30 mL |
| 2 tbsp | olive oil | 30 mL |
| 1 | garlic clove, finely chopped | 1 |
| 1 tsp | Tabasco sauce (optional) | 5 mL |
| ½ tsp | dried thyme or basil | 2 mL |

## ORIENTAL MARINADE

| ¼ cup | hoisin sauce | 50 mL |
| ¼ cup | soy or teriyaki sauce | 50 mL |
| 2 tbsp | honey or maple syrup | 30 mL |
| 1 tbsp | grated fresh ginger | 15 mL |
| 2 | garlic cloves, finely chopped | 2 |
| 1 tsp | Sambal Oelek* or chili paste (optional) | 5 mL |

* Sambal Oelek is a type of sauce made from hot peppers, available in Asian specialty food stores.

## DIJON MUSTARD MARINADE

| ¼ cup | mayonnaise | 50 mL |
| 3 tbsp | Dijon mustard | 45 mL |
| ¼ cup | chopped shallots | 50 mL |
| 2 tbsp | fresh lemon or lime juice | 30 mL |
| ½ tsp | salt | 2 mL |
| ½ tsp | dried thyme | 2 mL |
| ½ tsp | dried oregano | 2 mL |
| 1 | garlic clove, finely chopped | 1 |

## GREEK-STYLE MARINADE

| 2 tbsp | fresh lemon or lime juice | 30 mL |
| ½ tsp | salt | 2 mL |
| ½ tsp | pepper | 2 mL |
| ¼ tsp | ground cumin | 1 mL |
| ¼ tsp | oregano | 1 mL |
| 2 | garlic cloves, finely chopped | 2 |

## BEER MARINADE

| 11 oz | beer | 340 mL |
| ¼ cup | olive oil | 50 mL |
| 2 tbsp | soy sauce | 30 mL |
| 1 tbsp | chopped fresh parsley | 15 mL |
| | juice of 1 lemon | |

# RICH BROWN
# CHICKEN STOCK

*Preparation time: 10 minutes*
*Cooking time: 3 hours*
*Makes about 10 cups (2.5 L)*

| | | |
|---|---|---|
| 3 lbs | raw chicken bones | 1.5 kg |
| 2 | onions | 2 |
| 1 | celery stalk | 1 |
| 1 | large carrot | 1 |
| 1 | leek, green leaves only | 1 |
| 2 | large tomatoes | 2 |
| 2 tbsp | tomato paste | 30 mL |
| 1 | bouquet garni (see p. 165) | 1 |
| | water | |

- Preheat oven to 500°F (260°C).
- Place bones in a roasting pan and roast 25 to 30 minutes, or until well browned.
- Meanwhile, coarsely chop vegetables. When bones are browned, add vegetables and tomato paste to pan. Roast 4 or 5 minutes in oven.
- Transfer bones and vegetables to a large stock pot. Skim fat from roasting pan and place pan on stove top over high heat. Stir in 2 cups (500 mL) cold water, scraping bottom of pan, and bring to a boil.
- Pour contents of roasting pan over bones in stock pot. Add enough water to cover bones completely. Add bouquet garni and bring to a boil.
- Let simmer over low heat 2½ to 3 hours, skimming regularly, or until stock is a rich golden-brown color. Strain, let cool and refrigerate, covered, for later use.

# LIGHT CHICKEN STOCK

*Preparation time: 15 minutes*
*Cooking time: 3 hours*
*Makes about 10 cups (2.5 L)*

| | | |
|---|---|---|
| 3 lbs | raw chicken bones | 1.5 kg |
| 2 | onions | 2 |
| 2 | celery stalks | 2 |
| 1 | large carrot | 1 |
| 1 | leek, green part only | 1 |
| 2 tbsp | butter | 30 mL |
| 12 cups | water | 3 L |
| 1 | bouquet garni* | |

- Put bones in a pot and rinse under cold running water.
- Chop vegetables coarsely. Melt butter in a large saucepan; add vegetables and cook, covered, over medium-low heat 6 to 8 minutes.
- Add bones, water and bouquet garni. Bring to a boil over high heat. Lower heat and let simmer 2½ to 3 hours, skimming regularly.
- Strain, let cool and refrigerate, covered, for later use.

*For a flavorful bouquet garni: Cut a celery stalk in half crosswise. Between the two pieces, layer 1 sprig each of parsley, thyme, basil, and tarragon. Add 1 bay leaf, 1 crushed garlic clove, 2 whole cloves, and 10 peppercorns. Tie bundle together with kitchen string or in a piece of cheesecloth.*

# BECHAMEL SAUCE

*Preparation time: 5 minutes*
*Cooking time: 15 minutes*

| | | |
|---|---|---|
| 2 tbsp | butter | 30 mL |
| ½ | onion, chopped | ½ |
| 4 tbsp | all-purpose flour | 60 mL |
| 2 cups | hot milk | 500 mL |
| | pinch of nutmeg | |
| | salt and white pepper | |

- Melt butter in a saucepan over medium heat. Lower heat, add onion and cook 2 minutes. Stir in flour and cook 1 minute.
- Gradually add milk, whisking constantly. Season with salt and pepper; add nutmeg. Cook over low heat 8 to 10 minutes, stirring occasionally.
- Strain sauce into a bowl. Cover surface directly with waxed paper and let cool before refrigerating. Sauce will keep up to 3 days in refrigerator.

# BASIC PINK SAUCE

*Preparation time: 10 minutes*
*Cooking time: 30 minutes*
*Makes 3 cups (750 mL)*

| | | |
|---|---|---|
| 2 tbsp | olive oil | 30 mL |
| 2 tbsp | finely chopped shallots | 30 mL |
| 2 tbsp | finely chopped garlic | 30 mL |
| I cup | dry white wine | 250 mL |
| I | can crushed tomatoes (28 oz/796 mL) | I |
| I½ cups | chicken stock | 375 mL |
| I tsp | *each* dried oregano and basil | 5 mL |
| I | bouquet garni* | I |
| I tbsp | cornstarch dissolved in water | 15 mL |
| ½ cup | table cream (15%) | 125 mL |
| | salt and pepper | |

- Heat oil in a saucepan over medium heat. Add shallots and garlic; cook 3 minutes.
- Add wine, tomatoes, stock, oregano, basil and bouquet garni; season with salt and pepper.
- Cover and let simmer about 25 minutes over low heat. Remove bouquet garni and add dissolved cornstarch. Add cream and heat through just before serving.

*To make a simple bouquet garni, tie together 2 or 3 sprigs of parsley, I sprig of thyme and 2 or 3 bay leaves.

# TASTY TOMATO SAUCE

*Preparation time: 10 minutes*
*Cooking time: 3 hours*
*Makes 4 cups (1 L)*

| | | |
|---|---|---|
| 2 | large onions, finely chopped | 2 |
| 2 tbsp | olive oil | 30 mL |
| 4 | garlic cloves, finely chopped | 4 |
| 4 lbs | fresh plum tomatoes or 4 cans (28 oz/796 ml *each*) Italian tomatoes | 2 kg |
| 1 | sprig fresh thyme | 1 |
| 1 | bay leaf | 1 |
| 1 | sprig fresh parsley | 1 |
| 10 to 12 | whole peppercorns | 10 to 12 |
| | salt | |

- Heat oil in large saucepan. Add onions and cook over low heat, stirring constantly, until tender but not browned.
- Add garlic; continue cooking 2 to 3 minutes. Add whole tomatoes.
- Bundle herbs and peppercorns together in a piece of cheesecloth. Add to saucepan and season with salt.
- Let simmer, uncovered, over low heat about 3 hours, stirring frequently.

# BASIL PESTO

*Preparation time: 15 minutes*
*Makes 3 cups (750 mL)*

| | | |
|---|---|---|
| 2 | bunches fresh basil | 2 |
| ½ | bunch fresh parsley | ½ |
| 4 | garlic cloves, finely chopped | 4 |
| 1¼ cups | olive oil | 300 mL |
| ½ cup | grated Romano cheese | 125 mL |
| ½ cup | pine nuts | 125 mL |

- Remove stems from basil and parsley. Wash leaves well; spin or pat dry.
- Place leaves, garlic, oil, cheese and pine nuts in food processor or blender. Process until fairly smooth.
- Serve immediately or store in an airtight container up to 1 week in the refrigerator.

**Note:** *For longer storage, freeze pesto sauce in jars or in ice cube trays (each cube makes 1 serving).*

# DESSERTS

What came first, the chicken or the egg? Needless to say that when it comes to dessert, the egg takes the cake!

In this chapter you'll find special desserts to round off special meals, as well as quick and easy delights to satisfy that sweet tooth any day of the week. From *Pecan Brownies with Chocolate Frosting* to *Fresh Fruit Custard Pie*, these recipes are all simple and delicious!

# PINEAPPLE
# UPSIDE-DOWN CAKE

*Preparation time: 30 minutes*
*Cooking time: 1 hour*
*10 servings*

| | | |
|---|---|---|
| ¾ cup | softened butter | 175 mL |
| ½ cup | brown sugar | 125 mL |
| 1 | can pineapple slices (14 oz/398 mL), drained | 1 |
| ¾ cup | granulated sugar | 175 mL |
| 2 | eggs | 2 |
| 2 tsp | vanilla extract | 10 mL |
| 1½ cups | all-purpose flour | 375 mL |
| 1 tsp | baking powder | 5 mL |
| 1 tsp | baking soda | 5 mL |
| ¼ tsp | salt | 1 mL |
| ½ cup | buttermilk | 125 mL |

- Preheat oven to 350°F (180°C). Grease a 9-inch (23 cm) springform cake pan. Place pan on top of 2 layers of aluminum foil, folding foil up around pan.

- In a small saucepan over medium heat, cook ¼ cup (50 mL) butter with brown sugar, stirring constantly until mixture starts to boil. Remove from heat and pour into prepared pan. Arrange pineapple slices over sauce so that they overlap. Set aside.

- In a medium bowl, beat together remaining ½ cup (125 mL) butter and granulated sugar until fluffy. Add eggs and vanilla; beat well.

- Sift together flour, baking powder, baking soda, ginger and salt. Gradually add to egg mixture, alternating with buttermilk. Stir until smooth.

- Pour batter evenly over pineapple slices. Bake 50 to 60 minutes, or until toothpick inserted in center comes out clean.

- Run sharp knife around edges of cake to detach from pan. Release spring of pan. Place serving plate upside-down over pan. Turn plate and pan over. Let stand a few minutes to allow caramel to soak into cake, then gently remove pan. Serve with ice cream, if desired.

# PECAN BROWNIES
## WITH CHOCOLATE FROSTING

**Preparation time: 20 minutes**
**Cooking time: 35 minutes**
**Makes 12 to 16**

| | | |
|---|---|---|
| 6 oz | semi-sweet chocolate (6 squares) | 180 g |
| ¼ cup | butter | 50 mL |
| 2 | eggs | 2 |
| ½ cup | granulated sugar | 125 mL |
| 1 tsp | vanilla extract | 5 mL |
| ½ cup | all-purpose flour | 125 mL |
| ½ tsp | baking powder | 2 mL |
| ⅓ cup | chopped toasted pecans | 75 mL |

**Frosting:**

| | | |
|---|---|---|
| 3½ oz | semi-sweet chocolate (3½ squares) | 100 g |
| ¼ cup | sour cream | 50 mL |

- Preheat oven to 350°F (180°C). Grease an 8-inch (20 cm) square baking pan.

- Melt chocolate and butter together in the top of a double boiler or in the microwave. Set aside.

- Meanwhile, with electric mixer, beat together eggs, sugar and vanilla. Add melted chocolate and mix well.

- Stir in flour, baking powder and nuts. Pour batter into prepared pan. Bake 35 minutes, or until a toothpick inserted in center comes out clean. Let cool.

- Meanwhile, to make frosting, melt chocolate in top of double boiler. Stir in cream until smooth. Spread over brownies before serving.

## LEMON MAGIC PUDDING

*Preparation time: 10 minutes*
*Cooking time: 35 minutes*
*4 servings*

| | | |
|---|---|---|
| 3 | eggs, separated | 3 |
| ½ cup | granulated sugar | 125 mL |
| ⅓ cup | all-purpose flour | 75 mL |
| ¼ tsp | salt | 1 mL |
| 2 tsp | grated lemon zest | 10 mL |
| ¼ cup | fresh lemon juice | 50 mL |
| 1 tbsp | butter, melted | 15 mL |
| ¾ cup | milk | 175 mL |

- Preheat oven to 350°F (180°C).
- Beat egg whites until stiff peaks form.
- In separate bowl, stir together sugar, flour and salt. Whisk in lemon zest, lemon juice, butter, milk and egg yolks.
- Gently fold egg whites into lemon mixture until smooth. Pour into greased 4-cup (1 L) baking dish.
- Place baking dish in larger pan. Pour 1 inch (2.5 cm) hot water around baking dish. Bake for 35 to 40 minutes or until top is lightly browned. Serve warm or cold.

# RUM BABAS

**Preparation time: 30 minutes**
**Standing time: 1½ hours**
**Cooking time: 20 minutes**
**8 servings**

| | | |
|---|---|---|
| 2 cups | all-purpose flour, sifted | 500 mL |
| 3 tbsp | granulated sugar | 45 mL |
| 1½ tbsp | quick acting yeast | 22 mL |
| 4 | eggs, beaten (at room temperature) | 4 |
| ¼ cup | hot milk | 50 mL |
| 3 tbsp | melted butter | 45 mL |

**Syrup:**

| | | |
|---|---|---|
| 2 cups | water | 500 mL |
| 1¼ cups | granulated sugar | 300 mL |
| ⅓ cup | rum | 75 mL |

- In a medium bowl, stir together flour, 3 tbsp (45 mL) sugar and yeast. Add beaten eggs. Mix well.
- Add hot milk and melted butter. Stir until batter is soft and sticky.
- Grease eight ½-cup (125 mL) ramekins and divide batter evenly among them. Cover ramekins with waxed paper.
- Let batter rise in a warm place until doubled in volume, about 1½ hours.
- Preheat oven to 400°F (200°C). Bake babas on center rack 10 minutes. Lower temperature to 325°F (160°C) and continue baking 10 to 15 minutes or until golden.
- Meanwhile, prepare syrup. Place water, sugar and rum in saucepan. Cook over low heat, stirring occasionally, until sugar dissolves. Let cool.
- When babas are done, remove from oven and run sharp knife around edges to detach them from ramekins. Remove and let cool, pouring a little syrup over each baba every few minutes. Let syrup soak in then add more.

In a medium bowl, stir together flour, sugar and yeast. Add beaten eggs.

Add hot milk and melted butter. Stir until batter is soft and sticky.

Divide batter evenly among eight ramekins.

Cover ramekins with waxed paper.

Let batter rise in a warm place until doubled in volume.

Pour a little syrup over baked babas every few minutes. Let syrup soak in then add more.

# FRUIT AND NUT LOAF

***Preparation time: 20 minutes***
***Cooking time: 1 hour***
***Makes 1 loaf***

| | | |
|---|---|---|
| ½ cup | softened butter | 125 mL |
| 1 cup | granulated sugar | 250 mL |
| 2 | eggs | 2 |
| 1½ cups | sour cream | 375 mL |
| 1 cup | chopped pecans | 250 mL |
| ⅓ cup | coarsely chopped dates | 75 mL |
| ⅓ cup | coarsely chopped dried apricots | 75 mL |
| 1 tsp | grated orange zest | 5 mL |
| 2 cups | all-purpose flour | 500 mL |
| 1 tsp | baking soda | 5 mL |
| ½ tsp | baking powder | 2 mL |
| ½ tsp | salt | 2 mL |

- Preheat oven to 350°F (180°C). Grease a 5 x 9-inch (13 x 23 cm) loaf pan.
- With electric beater, beat together butter and sugar in a large bowl until fluffy. Add eggs, one at a time, beating after each addition.
- Stir in sour cream, pecans, dates, apricots and orange zest.
- Sift together remaining ingredients and gently fold into egg mixture; mix well.
- Pour batter into prepared pan. Bake 1 hour, or until a toothpick inserted in center comes out clean.

## FRESH FRUIT CUSTARD PIE

*Preparation time: 10 minutes*
*Cooking time: 40 minutes*
*Chilling time: 2 hours*
*8 servings*

| | | |
|---|---|---|
| 4 | eggs | 4 |
| ½ cup | granulated sugar | 125 mL |
| ½ tsp | vanilla extract | 2 mL |
| 1½ cups | milk, warmed | 375 mL |
| 1 | unbaked 9-inch (23 cm) pie shell | 1 |
| ¼ tsp | ground nutmeg | 1 mL |
| 1 | kiwi fruit, peeled and thinly sliced | 1 |
| 6 | fresh strawberries, halved | 6 |
| 1 | can mandarin orange segments (10 oz/284 mL), drained | 1 |
| | pinch of salt | |

- Preheat oven to 400°F (200°C). In a large bowl, whisk together eggs, sugar and salt.
- Combine vanilla extract and milk. Gradually stir into egg mixture.
- Pour into pie shell and sprinkle with nutmeg. Bake 10 minutes, then reduce heat to 350°F (180°C). Bake 30 minutes longer, or until toothpick inserted in center comes out clean. Remove from oven and let cool.
- Place overlapping kiwi slices in center of pie. Make a circle of strawberries around the kiwi then arrange tangerine segments along the outer edge. Chill in refrigerator at least 2 hours before serving.

# MAPLE WALNUT TARTS

*Preparation time: 15 minutes*
*Chilling time: 30 minutes*
*Cooking time: 20 minutes*
*Makes 12 tarts*

## Flaky Pastry:

| | | |
|---|---|---|
| 2 cups | all-purpose flour | 500 mL |
| 2 tbsp | granulated sugar | 30 mL |
| ½ tsp | salt | 2 mL |
| ¼ tsp | baking powder | 1 mL |
| ½ cup | cold butter, cut in pieces | 125 mL |
| ⅓ cup | vegetable shortening, at room temperature | 75 mL |
| ½ cup | ice-cold water (approx.) | 125 mL |

## Walnut Filling:

| | | |
|---|---|---|
| 3 | eggs | 3 |
| 1 cup | maple syrup | 250 mL |
| ¾ cup | packed brown sugar | 175 mL |
| 2 tbsp | butter, melted | 30 mL |
| 1 tsp | vanilla extract | 5 mL |
| 1 cup | coarsely chopped walnuts | 250 mL |

- In medium bowl, combine flour, granulated sugar, salt and baking powder. Cut in butter and shortening until mixture is crumbly.

- Add ice water 2 tbsp (30 mL) at a time, mixing with a fork until dough holds together but is not sticky.

- Press mixture into 2 flat rounds. Wrap in waxed paper and refrigerate 30 minutes.

- Meanwhile, beat together eggs, maple syrup, brown sugar, melted butter and vanilla.

- Preheat oven to 425°F (220°). On lightly floured board, roll pastry rounds to ⅛-inch (3 mm) thickness. Cut into 5-inch (12 cm) circles. Roll scraps of dough and cut again.

- Line twelve 3½-inch (9 cm) tart pans with pastry. Divide walnuts equally between tart shells. Pour maple syrup mixture over walnuts.

- Bake 20 to 25 minutes, or until pastry is golden and filling is just set. Let cool 15 minutes before removing from pans. Serve warm or at room temperature.

# BAKED APPLE
## SURPRISE

*Preparation time: 40 minutes*
*Cooking time: 25 minutes*
*6 servings*

| | | |
|---|---|---|
| 6 | Golden Delicious apples | 6 |
| ⅓ cup | cream cheese | 75 mL |
| ⅓ cup | brown sugar | 75 mL |
| 2 tbsp | toasted slivered almonds | 30 mL |
| ½ cup | raisins (optional) | 125 mL |
| 14 oz | frozen puff pastry (thawed) | 400 g |
| I | egg, beaten | I |
| | cinnamon to taste | |

- Preheat oven to 400°F (200°C). Grease a large baking sheet. Peel and core apples.

- Combine cream cheese, sugar, cinnamon, almonds and raisins. Stuff apples with mixture.

- Roll out pastry on a floured work surface. Cut into six 8-inch (20 cm) squares.

- Place 1 apple in center of each pastry square. Fold up sides and seal. Brush all over with beaten egg.

- Arrange apples on baking sheet. Bake 25 minutes or until golden-brown.

# CHOCOLATE RASPBERRY TORTE

*Preparation time: 15 minutes*
*Baking time: 35 minutes*
*8 servings*

| | | |
|---|---|---|
| 4 | eggs, separated | 4 |
| ½ cup | granulated sugar | 125 mL |
| 3 tbsp | unsweetened cocoa powder, sifted | 45 mL |
| ¼ cup | dry white breadcrumbs | 50 mL |
| ½ cup | ground almonds | 125 mL |
| ¼ cup | raspberry jam | 50 mL |
| I cup | heavy cream (35%), whipped | 250 mL |
| | fresh raspberries | |

- Preheat oven to 350°F (180°C).
- In a bowl, beat egg whites until stiff peaks form.
- In large bowl, beat egg yolks and sugar until thick and light. In a separate bowl, combine cocoa powder, breadcrumbs and almonds. Fold into egg yolks.
- Fold beaten egg whites into egg yolk mixture in 2 batches.
- Pour batter into greased 9-inch (23 cm) springform cake pan. Bake 35 to 40 minutes, until top springs back when gently touched.
- Place upside down on wire rack and let cool completely. Loosen edges with knife to remove from pan.
- Spread jam evenly over torte. Serve topped with whipped cream and raspberries.

# ORANGE
# CHIFFON CAKE

***Preparation time: 20 minutes***
***Cooking time: 1 hour***
***10 to 12 servings***

| | | |
|---|---|---|
| 2 cups | sifted cake flour | 500 mL |
| 1½ cups | granulated sugar | 375 mL |
| 1 tbsp | baking powder | 15 mL |
| ½ tsp | salt | 2 mL |
| 8 | eggs, at room temperature, separated | 8 |
| ½ cup | vegetable oil | 125 mL |
| ½ cup | milk | 125 mL |
| 1 tsp | grated orange zest | 5 mL |
| ¼ cup | fresh orange juice | 50 mL |
| ½ tsp | cream of tartar | 2 mL |

**Orange Icing:**

| | | |
|---|---|---|
| 1½ cups | icing sugar | 375 mL |
| 1 tsp | grated orange zest | 5 mL |
| 2-3 tbsp | orange juice | 30-45 mL |

- Preheat oven to 325°F (160°C).

- In large bowl, sift together flour, granulated sugar, baking powder and salt. Make a well in center. Add egg yolks, oil, milk, 1 tsp (5 mL) orange zest and ¼ cup (50 mL) juice. Stir until smooth.

- Beat egg whites together with cream of tartar until stiff peaks form. Gently fold ⅓ of whites into flour mixture. Fold in remaining egg whites.

- Pour batter into nonstick Bundt® pan. Bake 1 hour, or until top springs back when gently touched. Place upside down on wire rack to cool.

- Meanwhile, mix together all icing ingredients until smooth. Spread over cooled cake and serve.

*In large bowl, sift together flour, granulated sugar, baking powder and salt. Make a well in center.*

*Add egg yolks, oil, milk, orange zest and juice. Stir until smooth.*

Beat egg whites together with cream of tartar until stiff peaks form.

Gently fold ⅓ of whites into flour mixture. Fold in remaining egg whites.

Pour batter into nonstick Bundt® pan.

# COCONUT
# MACAROONS

*Preparation time: 15 minutes*
*Cooking time: 20 minutes*
*Makes about 4 dozen*

| 2 cups | sweetened flaked coconut | 500 mL |
|---|---|---|
| 1 cup | granulated sugar | 250 mL |
| 3 tbsp | all-purpose flour | 45 mL |
| 4 | egg whites, at room temperature | 4 |
| ¼ tsp | almond or vanilla extract pinch of salt | 1 mL |

## Variations:

**Chocolate Coconut Macaroons:** Melt 2 oz (60 g) semi-sweet chocolate over hot water. Drizzle over surface of baked and cooled cookies.

**Nutty Macaroons:** Reduce coconut to 1½ cups (375 mL) and add ½ cup (125 mL) chopped almonds or hazelnuts to coconut mixture. Garnish with whole nuts before baking.

- Preheat oven to 325°F (160°C). Combine coconut, ¼ cup (50 mL) sugar and flour; set aside.
- Beat egg whites with almond extract and salt until soft peaks form. Gradually add remaining sugar, 2 tbsp (30 mL) at a time, beating until stiff and glossy. Fold in coconut mixture.
- Drop tablespoons (15 mL) of batter onto cookie sheets lined with parchment paper or aluminum foil. Bake 20 minutes, or until firm and lightly browned.
- Let cool on paper, then peel off carefully.

# CHOCOLATE PRUNE AND NUT CAKE

**Preparation time: 20 minutes**
**Cooking time: 40 minutes**
**9 servings**

| | | |
|---|---|---|
| ½ cup | butter | 125 mL |
| ¾ cup | brown sugar | 175 mL |
| 2 | large eggs | 2 |
| 1½ cups | all-purpose flour | 375 mL |
| 1 tsp | baking powder | 5 mL |
| ¼ cup | chopped almonds | 50 mL |
| 4 oz | semi-sweet chocolate (4 squares), melted | 120 g |
| 1 cup | pitted prunes, finely chopped | 250 mL |
| | pinch of salt | |

- Preheat oven to 350°F (180°C). Grease a 5 x 9-inch (13 x 23 cm) loaf pan.

- Melt butter in a medium saucepan over medium heat. Remove pan from heat, and stir in brown sugar. Beat in remaining ingredients one at a time.

- Pour batter into prepared pan. Bake 45 to 50 minutes, or until a toothpick inserted in center comes out clean. Let cool on wire rack before removing from pan.

- Slice and serve with ice cream, chocolate sauce and raspberries, if desired.

# ZUCCHINI CAKE
# WITH COCONUT GLAZE

*Preparation time: 15 minutes*
*Cooking time: 40 minutes*
*8 servings*

| | | |
|---|---|---|
| 1¼ cups | all-purpose flour | 300 mL |
| 1 tsp | baking powder | 5 mL |
| ⅛ tsp | salt | 0.5 mL |
| ½ tsp | baking soda | 2 mL |
| ½ cup | brown sugar | 125 mL |
| 1½ cups | grated unpeeled zucchini | 375 mL |
| ½ cup | vegetable oil | 125 mL |
| 2 | eggs, lightly beaten | 2 |
| ½ cup | sour cream | 125 mL |
| | heavy cream (35%) | |

**Coconut Glaze:**

| | | |
|---|---|---|
| 1 cup | brown sugar | 250 mL |
| ¼ cup | 35% or 15% cream | 50 mL |
| ½ cup | butter | 125 mL |
| 1½ cups | shredded coconut | 375 mL |

- Preheat oven to 350°F (180°C). In a large bowl, sift together flour, baking powder, salt, baking soda and cinnamon. Stir in brown sugar and grated zucchini.
- Combine oil, beaten eggs and sour cream. Stir into flour mixture.
- Grease and lightly flour an 8-inch (20 cm) round cake pan at least 2½ inches (6 cm) deep. Pour batter into pan. Bake 40 minutes or until toothpick inserted in center comes out clean.
- Meanwhile, combine coconut glaze ingredients in a saucepan and cook over low heat, stirring constantly, until sugar dissolves.
- When cake is done, spread coconut glaze evenly over cake and let cool. Serve with heavy cream.

Stir brown sugar and grated zucchini into flour mixture.

Combine oil, beaten eggs and sour cream.

Stir egg mixture into flour mixture.

*Grease and lightly flour an 8-inch (20 cm) round cake pan at least 2½ inches (6 cm) deep.*

*Pour batter into pan.*

*When cake is done, spread coconut glaze evenly over cake and let cool.*

# APPLE AND SPICE
# BREAD PUDDING

**Preparation time: 10 minutes**
**Chilling time: 4 hours**
**Cooking time: 45 minutes**
**8 servings**

| | | |
|---|---|---|
| 2 tbsp | butter | 30 mL |
| 2 | medium apples, cored and chopped | 2 |
| 3 cups | day-old white or wholewheat bread cubes | 750 mL |
| ½ cup | raisins | 125 mL |
| 2 | eggs | 2 |
| 2 cups | milk | 500 mL |
| ⅓ cup | packed brown sugar | 75 mL |
| 1 tsp | vanilla extract | 5 mL |
| ½ tsp | ground cinnamon | 2 mL |
| ¼ tsp | ground nutmeg | 1 mL |

- Melt butter in a small saucepan over medium heat. Stir in apples. Cover and cook about 5 minutes, stirring occasionally, until slightly softened.

- Grease a shallow 6-cup (1.5 L) baking dish. Add apples, bread cubes and raisins. Mix well.

- In a medium bowl, beat together eggs, milk, brown sugar, vanilla, cinnamon and nutmeg until smooth. Pour over apple mixture. Cover and refrigerate at least 4 hours.

- Preheat oven to 350°F (180°C). Bake pudding 40 to 45 minutes or until knife inserted in center comes out clean. Serve hot, warm or chilled.

# CHERRY CLAFOUTIS

**Preparation time: 15 minutes**
**Cooking time: 35 minutes**
**8 servings**

| | | |
|---|---|---|
| 1 | can Bing cherries (14 oz/397 g), drained and pitted | 1 |
| 5 | eggs | 5 |
| ⅓ cup | granulated sugar | 75 mL |
| ⅔ cup | all-purpose flour | 150 mL |
| ¼ cup | melted butter, warm | 50 mL |
| 1 tsp | vanilla extract | 5 mL |

- Preheat oven to 400°F (200°C). Arrange cherries in a greased 10-inch (25 cm) quiche pan or pie plate.
- In a bowl, beat eggs about 3 minutes with electric beater. Gradually beat in sugar and flour.
- Add butter and vanilla. Mix well. Pour mixture over cherries.
- Bake 35 minutes, or until a toothpick inserted in center comes out clean. Let stand 5 minutes before serving.

# INDEX

## S

## T

## V

## W

## Z